The N   Achieving
Your Dreams

Sheldon D. Newton

Diligence The Master Key To Achieving Your Dreams
© 2014
Sheldon D. Newton

Sheldon D. Newton
P. O. Box N. 10257
Nassau, Bahamas
Email: sheldond.newton@gmail.com

A JCCMI Production

Contents

ACKNOWLEDGEMENTS

I would like to thank the following people for their help in the preparation of this manuscript: My wife, Jennifer Monique for helping with the editing. Thanks beautiful.

Deborah Moore (Thanks for being my proof-reader. You are such a blessing), Devin Francis (what a beautiful cover bro).

Dedication

I would like to dedicate this book to my son, Sheldon Jr and my daughter, Jasma Jenaris. Never, ever limit yourselves. With God all things are truly possible. Always remember that.

And to all of those who can hear their destinies calling them from within. Rise up and be all you can truly be.

Preface

As a person who desires to add value to people's lives through the practical application of principles and truth, I believe there is worth and great potential in every person on earth. You have the God-given ability to accomplish tremendous things, to reach your goals and to fulfill your dreams. Now one might say, "Well look at this. Another book on reaching your goals. I have read many of them and still have not realized any of my goals. Why should I read this one?" The answer is simply because it may be the missing link as to why things have not happened for you as you desired.

The question then is, what solution can I offer you that may be necessary for you to accomplish the dream in your heart, right? The answer is within the pages of this book. But permit to say that after much observation, counseling and prayer for many years, I have come to the realization that diligence is the master key to attaining your goals.

Have you made plans you desire to achieve? Maybe you have made New Year's resolutions over and over again, only to realize at the end of the year how little you got done. If that is your plight, I have written this book to show you the vital principle which successful people in each arena of life used to get where they desired to go. Once you learn this key, you can open the doors you need to walk through and experience the joy of hopes fulfilled and dreams becoming a reality.

You can get the kind of job you want. You can become that person you were destined to be. You can change. You can accomplish those things you have within your heart. You can attain your dreams. You can, you can, you can. This book will show you how. So, get ready. Your life is about to change for the better. Adventures await you. So read on.

Chapter One
Diligence is the Master Key to Greatness

There is only one way to accomplish your goals. And that is by diligently pursuing them, doing so relentlessly with determination and fortitude.

Diligence is the golden key of all worthy achievements, for it is the power to consistently and persistently engage our energies and efforts to their attainment. To be diligent implies giving constant, careful, steady attention to something. In other words, it means to know what you want, go after what you want and refuse to stop until you get what you want. This is the attitude that wins in life.

Everyone who has done something deserving of attention has employed diligence to make it happened. No one can be truly successful without this powerful force. Many of us make new goals every year. We call them New Year's Resolutions. What is interesting however is that some of these goals are the same ones we made the previous year, or even before that. We never attained them. They did not become reality. Amidst the fact that some goals and dreams take years to fully manifest, one cannot help to think that the obvious reason most goals are not realized is because the actions and sustained actions necessary to bring them to fruition are not implemented effectively and sufficiently.

Indeed it would be startling to do a survey as to how many of us have failed to realize our dreams, not because the timing was not right, but because we simply did not give our all and pursue them. In other words, we were not diligent.

Ask any successful person and they will tell you they won in life because they determined to do so. They will share with you the hurdles they had to over-come, the giants they had to slay, the challenges they had to face and the pressures they had to endure. They will convince you of, not just their victories, but also of their struggles, as they learned to push pass things which otherwise may have convinced them to stop, and just when things looked the worst, that extra push, that extra action, that determined drive made the difference and brought them into their desired place in life. No one wins without being determined to do so. Diligence is the master key to achievement.

Your goal is within reach if you are prepared to do what it takes, and do enough of what it takes to make it a reality. You actually have more for you than against you. The Great Creator of the universe is for your success. He is willing to help you and empower you so that you can see your dreams come to pass. But in the final analysis, whether you succeed or not is up to you. The choices you make determine your fate.

This is a point some do not want to accept and would argue with. After all, it is human nature to blame all seemingly bad happenings on God, regardless of the part that we had to play in the ordeal. The truth of the matter is that the Sovereign One so desires for us to win in life, He has provided the ways and means for us to overcome our negative situations and win in life.

So you and I have more for us than against us. We can see our dreams become a reality. We can enjoy life, experiencing the sweet taste of conquest and victory over and over again. We are able to defeat our giants, literally bursting through every limitation that presents itself, making a mark in this world which is never erased or forgotten. The question is not, "Can my dreams come true?" The real question is, "Am I prepared, with God's help, to do what it takes to see them happen?"

Successful people apply diligence to their goals and dreams. That is why they win in life.

Chapter Two
Diligence Involves Planning

Someone made the following statement years ago. I do not know who the first person was to say this, but I heard it from my former pastor years ago and it stuck with me: "If you fail to plan, you plan to fail."

This is so true. Planning is the meticulous formulation of setting realistic, workable and attainable goals which when implemented can bring a person to the realization of his or her dreams. To plan actually means that we have a vision of what we want and where we desire to go in life, so we are now busy devising the action steps necessary to get there. Planning is work, because we will have to, through prayer and consideration, use the minds the Creator blessed us with to look at where we desire to reach and how we are going to get there.

The first step to achieving anything is to ask ourselves, whether it is as individuals, or collectively as a group, where we ultimately want to end up. What do we want to do, be or have? What is your dream? Your dreams may be varied. You may have a dream for your life's occupation. You may have a dream for your family. You may have a dream. You may sense a God-given destiny and purpose for your life. Write it down. Write down what is in your heart to accomplish and attain as clearly as you can.

Write down your dreams for your life personally. Write down your vision for your future, your desires for your family. Write down what you would like to accomplish within a year, then within two years and carry your passion straight up to your tenth year, even beyond. Write down what you would like to do, what you desire to become. A good bit of advice along these lines is to take some time and think things through. Enquire of God, asking for His will, plan and purpose for your life. Everyone who comes into this world has a unique purpose for being here. The Creator knew you were coming, regardless of how you arrived, and devised a plan, a Divine destiny for your life, which is the only place where you will discover total satisfaction for being.

Take some time and consider carefully what you are here to do. Ask Him to reveal Himself and His purpose for you to you. Then, as different desires come into your heart, things which are good and noble, write them down, regardless of how far-fetched they seem. A true vision for your life will call you up to the place where it is. So of course, your dreams and desires may look as if they are impossible for you to attain. Write them down anyway. The "how" will appear.

Your dream at the moment may be that of losing some weight. Do not fear. This is a good dream. Your dream may be to have a flourishing bank account with money to give as well as to spend so that you and your family may enjoy life. Again, that is well. Your dreams may be of a spiritual nature. It may be that you desire to get close and even closer still to the Lord. Write that down. The purpose of writing down what you desire is to engage your mind. When you have a direction you want to go, your mind, like our modern day GPS systems, will diligently began to look for a way to reach your dreams.

You may be, and most likely are, like me, having dreams for your life, spiritually, mentally, physically, socially and financially. That is good. Write those down, and in the order of their importance to you. Write each dream on a different page in your dream or vision book. You will need to do this so that you can write your plans and intentions for how you will reach each one, and the timeline you will set for their various fulfillments.

After writing down your dreams, begin now to break each one down into goals. Goals are steps you will need to take as you head in the direction of your dreams. Goals are those places of achievements you must attain to in order to, in the end, stand in your dreams. So begin now to set workable goals. Write them down, one step after the other. Make sure that your goals are action steps which you can begin to immediately implement. This is important. You need goals you can start right away, while your enthusiasm to reach for your dreams is at an all time high.

So, if your desire is to save more money, a noteworthy goal is to have a bank account. Then you may need a job, something which can bring in income. You may need to start by saving ten dollars or even five dollars a week, or fifty dollars a month. The important thing is to begin where you are and work your way up.

Your dream may be to enjoy a better relationship with your spouse. You may have to set as your starting place that you will need to apologize for wrong behavior, or for harsh words which have been spoken over the years, which have deeply cut and wounded your spouse and therefore hurt your relationship. Do so and mean it when you say you are sorry. You may have to set aside special moments when the two of you can spend extra time together. I encourage husbands and wives from our church to get away and vacation together every so often. It really does make a difference in the marriage.

Maybe your dreams involve becoming a nurse, a policeman or policewoman. It may be that you desire to become a minister of the Gospel, a businessman, business woman or a singer. Perhaps your dream is simply to go back to school and finish your education. Whatever your dreams, make workable and achievable goals, steps which you can take right from where you are to get where you desire to be. Much of the time, the more detailed the plans, the better your chances to experience their reality.

Those who teach us how to plan our lives and our future say that planning is meticulous and can prove to be tiresome. Your mind will be working to see how you can arrive at your desired destination. Let it work as your servant. Much of the time however, when you run out of what to do next, if you are one who acknowledges God, the answer to the next step will appear when you are not even considering it. Take the time to make your plans diligently. It is one of the things winners do.

Chapter Three
Diligence involves Action

Proverbs 10:4
"He becometh poor that dealeth with a slack hand, but the hand of the diligent maketh rich."

Diligence is action.

It is the relentless pursuit of a person of vision. What separates the winners from those who never experience the sweetness of a fulfilled dream is action. Winners act. Those who do not act, for whatever reason, do not win. It is really that simple.

Someone may say, "But I acted. I did my part and nothing changed, nothing happened." But did you keep on acting? Did you persist in doing what you knew to do? Breakthrough is the result of consistent action. Show me an individual with talent who refuses to act, who dares not use his or her gift because of ignorance or fear of failure, and I will show you someone who, unless they change, will not get very far in life. Nothing happens without bold aggressive action.

A person may say, "I want to learn to play the piano." But wanting something without pursuing it will not make it a reality. Someone else may say, "I want to sing all over the world." What are you doing about it? And another still may cry, "I desire to be a teacher." Will you take the action steps which lead to the fulfillment of your desires? You can desire all day long and still not experience success. Who does not desire to win in life? I believe everyone thinks they do. But few actually become victorious because few take action.

What we must ask ourselves is, are we really desirous of attaining our goals and dreams, or are we just hoping that somehow, some way, they will manifest without our participation? After all, we actually pursue what we really want, don't we?

I know of a young man, rather handsome by the way, who had a dream of getting his car license so that he could legally drive on the road. Being a Christian, he dared not break the law of the land. He had to get his license. This was a worthy goal. However, the young man hesitated and procrastinated. He did not act on his goal. Instead, he prayed. Yes, that's right, prayed for years, petitioning God to help him get his license so that he could drive. He got married and even had children and still was asking God to help him get his license.

Now get this: he even brought a car from some friends of his, a nice baby-blue colored car. But alas, he had to have someone drive it to his home and park it for him, with him in the passenger seat, for he was not licensed to drive. He left home day by day, looking at his car, telling it, "Soon," leaving it parked while he went and caught the bus to work. In the evening he would continue petitioning God for some favor, some big break so that he would get his license to drive his car. Nothing happened.

He eventually ended up selling the car. He purchased another, and had a friend drive it by his home. He still could not drive it because he did not have a license. One day, he sat on his steps, and once again told God how he wanted his license so that he could drive his car. Then, and it seemed by revelation, the answer came from Heaven. It was transformational. It was enlightening. It was revolutionary. It seemed as if God spoke to the young man and said, "I do not have your license. The Ministry of Transport has it. Go to them and get it."

Wow. There it was. There was the answer that the young man needed was years. It was evident. It was a fact. It was something that was known. It was not a mystery. It was common sense. It did not even need to be prayed about. The answer was so obvious.

Why did he miss it? This we shall see in another chapter. But what is indeed amazing was that after the young man realized the foolishness and absurdity of praying in the manner he did, he went and got his license within two months. He could have had it from the age of eighteen. Instead, he got his license at the age of thirty. Because he refused to act, he suffered needlessly.

He took the driving test once and passed it. He thought about it later. Why did he wait so long? He felt stupid. He could have been driving from a long time ago. Why did he take so long to enjoy the privilege of driving himself and his family wherever they wanted to go, rather than always being dependent on others? The answer was simple. He did not drive because he did not have his license. He did not have his license because he did not act. He knew where it was. He did not need God to tell him. He knew what he needed to do to get it. Going to a driving school was a noteworthy ideal. But simply put, he did not have his license because he did not act on what he knew. Information alone was not enough to make his dream of being a licensed driver become a reality. Nothing happened until he acted.

"But who was this dummy, you may ask?" He should have known better. Why was he praying such an outrageous prayer? Well, to answer your question, I must admit that the dummy in this instance was the author of this book. As to why, instead of taking action, he just sat on the sidelines so to speak and prayed about something that he himself was responsible for doing, I will answer that when you answer this question: Are you acting on your goals or just praying and hoping they come to pass?

My friend, nothing happens until you do your part and act on your goals. Successful people diligently take action on their goals. That is why they win in life.

16

Chapter Four
Diligence Involves Becoming Consistent

Consistency is the key to accomplishing any worthy goal.

To be consistent simply means to keep at something until you get the result you desire. Just keep at it. It means to be constant and assiduous. In other words diligent.

Consistency describes the person who has dreams and goals and makes the firm, no turning around decision to pursue and stick to them making their desires a reality. He or she realizes and determines that the prize of experiencing their dream is worth going after, having weighed the price to be paid, and deciding that the objective is far more valuable than the cost. The sacrifices to be encountered and the challenges to be faced are deemed but a light matter, a small thing, when compared to reaching your destiny. Consistency is diligence in action.

Any coach in any sport, whether it be basketball, baseball, football or golf, will tell you that success in the various sports is dependent upon being consistent in practice. Those who attempt to teach us how to lose weight also speak of this necessary principle, which guarantees our success. They teach us the importance of eating the right foods and of exercising constantly, both of which cannot truly benefit us unless we become consistent in our instructed practices.

Many people do not enjoy financial stability and security because, regardless of how much money they amass, they have yet to learn about the importance of budgeting and allocation. This is true. You can make a lot of money and still be broke. Please do not misunderstand me. Making money is a good thing. It is needed to handle the affairs of this life. But

17

if you do not learn how to handle it right, you may end up living far below the life you and your family can and should enjoy.

I know what it is to be blessed financially, and then to be broke in a matter of a few days, or a few weeks. This is because after the blessing comes the responsibility of handling what we have been given or have been paid for our labor. Here is just a peek into what I am speaking about. You may make money, but if you do not save money consistently, then you will not be financially sound, regardless of how much you confess that you are rich. Old timers used to say, and I quote, "A fool and money don't mix."

You should give ten percent at the least to the work of the Lord where you are fed the truth of God's Word. God will bless the work of your hands if you practice this principle, trusting Him.

Then you need to learn how to handle and manage what is left. If you practice saving ten to twenty percent of what God brings into your hands, whether through the avenue of your job or otherwise, you will be astounded as to how much you will have in a year, five years, ten years, etc. This is a principle Joseph practiced in his day and literally was able to feed thousands. It is also a principle that experts in the financial realm teach as sound business sense. (Wonder where they got it)?

On the other hand, even if you make thousands, but save nothing, you will still be struggling financially year to year. Wise people teach us that if we save a percentage of what we make for ourselves, putting it up in a bank account or a bond fund, refusing to use it for foolish and unnecessary spending, our money will increase. Leave it, add to it and let it grow.

While I am not just speaking of finances, I believe that this example can prove profitable for anyone who adheres to and consistently practices it. This also teaches us the value of being constant in whatever we are pursuing.

18

Learning how to be consistent is well worth it. To be consistent is the sign of a diligent life. And if you and I are going to amount to anything in God or in our varied personal goals, we must take upon ourselves this worthy trait of diligence and determination and make it a part of our focus and daily routine. We must practice doing what we need to do daily to get the result we desire. This is true in relation to our dreams, career and natural goals, such as losing weight or saving money and also holds true in spiritual matters.

One of the most important lessons you will ever learn about being successful is that knowledge and information alone are not enough. Do not misunderstand me. We need knowledge. We need information. But information concerning losing weight without application of that information will never profit you. You must participate. You must get involved in your desired purpose for your dreams to come to pass.

If you desire to lose, you will have to eat better, drink water daily and exercise regularly. Now, eating right for one day, or even one week is good. But it is not enough if you need to lose weight and put off some pounds. You will have to practice doing these things constantly if they are to profit you. Eating good once will not do it. Exercising for a day will not do it. You must develop the habit of consistence.

Wanting something and wishing for it is not sufficient to bring it to you. You must show that you want it by diligently pursuing it daily. There is no other way to get something done but to apply yourself and do your part.

Think for a moment. Many of us have started in the direction of our dreams over and over again. Most likely, we began at the start of each New Year to endeavor to put some plan into action. However, most people have never reached their destination because they quit too soon. They were not consistent. Is this perhaps your story? Maybe you began a project, but because of fear, a lack of enthusiasm, a seeming lack of finances, or a negative remark from someone you respected, you stopped taking action on your set goals. It is time to pick your plans back up. It is time to once again diligently pursue your goals and experience the reality of a fulfilled dream.

Successful people diligently apply the force of consistency as they pursue their goals and dreams. That is why they win in life.

Chapter Five
Diligence Involves Focus

James 1:8 (AMP)
"[For being as he is] a man of two minds (hesitating, dubious, irresolute), [he is] unstable and unreliable and uncertain about everything [he thinks, feels, decides]."

Several years ago I had the rare privilege of sitting in the presence of a young multi-millionaire and hear him say a few words of wisdom which, if applied consistently, can transform any individual, regardless of their age, status in life or color. I was working for a company of which he was one of the principal owners. The part of the company I was attached to was holding a dinner for us and the aforementioned gentleman was present. As a group of the men were sitting together talking, and I among them, this brilliant young man, still in his forty's came over and sat with us, listening to our conversation, and maybe our fantasies of what it would take for us to win in life and become successful, even as he was.

Since we were only able to speak from theory, while he could talk from experience, I determined to get him involved in the conversation so we could, "pick his brain." I wanted to learn from one who had so defied the odds and knew what it was to overcome obstacles and hurdles, accomplishing so much at such a young age. Our time with him was brief, and yet he shared with us, prompted by my questions, a few truths which have and continue to inspire and motivate me to this very day. It is one of these wise sayings which I wish to impart to you in this particular chapter. I will share another soon, so please keep reading. He gave us golden nuggets which can transform any life. It is up to the individual to apply them and reap their enormous benefits.

I asked the young multi-millionaire how he was able to accomplish so much in such a short space of time. He was not apparently born wealthy. And yet, he had amassed riches and continues to do so, even right in the middle of a recession. He is prosperous. I wanted to know what had brought about his success. He answered me with one statement which, I guess in his estimation, said it all. It took me a long time to understand it. His reply was, and I quote, **"I'm a very focused man."**

I have meditated upon that phrase many times through the years. I still do. What does focus have to do with being successful in your endeavors? Why is it so necessary for those of us who desire to see our dreams become a reality? And what does it mean to be focused anyway?

I have discovered both by observation and experience that you must learn to focus if you truly desire to accomplish anything worthwhile.

To focus implies setting the mind upon some task, some desired end; a goal to attain, a dream to reach; and keeping it set there, to ensure that one keeps going in that direction. Focus is the powerful force and application which determines the following: I know what I desire; I can have what I desire; and by God's grace, I will have what I desire. I refuse to let people's opinions stop or hinder me. I will not allow my money or the lack thereof to stop me. I won't permit where I came from or my conditions at the present to hinder me. And I will not even allow me, my feelings, my up-bringing or my so-called weaknesses to block me.

This is so important to understand. Many people believe that their environment makes them who they are. "If I grew up in a poor neighborhood and all my people were poor, then I might assume that it was my lot in life.' Or, "None of my family is that educated. We are simply not smart folks, so how can I ascend and become a doctor or a lawyer or some attain any other seemingly high and noble profession?" The truth of the matter is that you can change either of those excuses whenever you want to.

Again, life is not left to fate. Whatever will be will not be if we make the right decisions in life, knowing what we want and staying focused upon achieving what we want with determination and persistent action. It has been proven time and time again that if you are willing enough and daring enough and focused enough, and if you believe strongly enough, you can rise above your circumstances and live a truly successful and satisfying life. It is the will of God that you stand in this earth as more than a conqueror. So you do not have to live defeated and conquered. Rise up and with His help seize your destiny. Great things are in store for us all, but it is the person who focuses upon his or her God-given dreams and goals who will win.

I have come to realize that failure in any endeavor is the result of not staying focus on the task at hand. The lesson that the young multi-millionaire shared with us on focus was and is the key to all achievement. Try to avoid and do away with all distractions and set your mind on the goal before you. Set it there and keep it set.

I once went to a Minister's Conference where I heard a man of God expound the Word of God and share from his personal experience how he had been able to do so much for the Kingdom of God. This particular preacher is known for his commitment to the things of God. And he is respected because he not only preaches the Bible, but he lives by the principles he preaches.

Being a teacher of the Word of God myself, I desired to glean from his wealth of experience in the ministry. Sure enough, he shared things he had learned through the years. And I felt so honored to be there to hear him. One of the things he impressed upon those of us who were there was to focus on what we knew the Lord had placed in our hearts to do. There it was again: **FOCUS.**

When a person is focused he or she determines to do what is necessary to get where they need to go. Focused people do not stay around those who are not going anywhere because they refuse to allow others to dampen their spirits or persuade them otherwise. Company matters. If you hang around people who are not valuing themselves and their time enough to make worthwhile goals and pursue them, they will attempt to lure you into their lack of zeal and may even tell you to forget what you want to do for it would never happen. It is often said that you cannot be a chicken and fly with the eagles. So, if your company, those you are constantly around, listening to for advice and counsel, are negative people, you will have to change sides.

Permit me to go a little further about focus. When we are focused upon our dreams and goals, meaning we know what we want, and where we desire to end up, we will have many distractions coming against us along the way. These seeming hindrances will come in the form of loved ones, as well as enemies who desire our hurt. But if we determine to stay with what we have set out to accomplish, refusing to be side-tracked, we will reach our haven of rest. The main thing is to keep the main thing before us.

If you desire to lose weight and be a particular size, the first thing you must do is decide how much weight you will need to lose to reach your dream size. Then you will have to determine how you are going to change your eating habits in order to make your dream a reality. You will have to exercise, and may need to enquire for professional help from those who work in both the weight loss industries as well as those who know something about doing different forms of exercise and weight lifting, or even aerobic dance. Knowledge is important.

After getting the information, you will need to set the time-line of when you will begin and at what time you intend on reaching your designated target. Now comes that moment when you must focus on the objective and take action. You must do this daily, assiduously, diligently. You cannot let up.

If you back off for a few days, those days may become weeks, months, years. Some of you know just what I am speaking about. If you do not practice consistency, you will fail in your objective.

So, you must focus if you want to taste the sweetness of victory. Stick with it. Stay at it. Keep on doing what you know you have to do to get the results you desire. I know that exercise for the first week or month may seem painful. But stay with it. Do not give up on your dream. Yes, your body, your unruly flesh may want to keep feeding on that junk food it always got. But remember that you cannot get the results you want doing the same things you always did. That is simply not possible.

Purpose in your heart and mind that you are in this until you get your results. **FOCUS, FOCUS, FOCUS.**

Someone may say, after a week, "You don't look like you are losing any weight. You might as well eat what you know you really want. Your diet or the changing of the way you eat is not working for you." Do not be side-tracked. Refuse to be discouraged. Keep at it. Your dream will become real if you do not give up.

Successful people are focused. That is why they win in life.

Chapter Six
Diligent People Refuse to Procrastinate

Procrastination has robbed more people of their God-ordained destiny than perhaps anything else. The habit and practice of continually putting off the important and necessary, while yielding to the trivial matters reveal that we are governed more by our feelings and fears than by true faith or even simple logic and common sense.

To procrastinate means to continually put off doing things which should be done when they should be our primary purpose and have our immediate attention. That is really what it is, is it not? It means according to Webster's Dictionary, to delay and postpone. It also means to drag your feet. What a description.

Are you putting off things you should be busy doing, probably engaging your time, energy and efforts into other things, just so that you do not have to deal with what you know you should be doing? Maybe you should be writing that manuscript for a book, or taking those piano lessons or guitar lessons so that you could publish your book or sing those songs which are bursting in your heart. Have you continued to take action and gotten your book printed or recorded some of your songs? No one will read your book if it is not out. No one will hear your songs if they are not sung.

Perhaps you have been putting off going back to school, to pursue the education you need to get you where you desire to go. It could be as simple as going to a bank to open a savings account so you can begin to save money. Or maybe you keep putting off other goals and dreams when you should be going after them. Regardless of the reasons why you preferred to deter from the pursuit of your dreams, than to pursue them, please note that they will not come to pass if you continue procrastinating.

I have learned that we, too many times, are our own worst enemy. We keep ourselves back and hinder our own progress. There is so much each one of us can accomplish if only we will steadily apply ourselves to our goals day by day, refusing to give ourselves the opportunity to persist in excuses. Maybe we think that things are not favorable for our goals to happen now. "When things get better," we say. But the perfect time may never come for us to implement our goals as we pursue our dreams. If we look at how things appear, we may never begin.

If you want to accomplish anything you will have to master procrastination. You will have to gain control of your feelings, muster up your courage and take massive action on your goals, pushing them as far as you can without letting up or caving in. You are the only one who can hold yourself back. So stop blaming others for your lack of boldness and make up your mind that you are going to live in the reality of your dream. Determined people win.

Do you remember the story I told of myself as it pertains to my driver's license? Of course you do. You may still be chuckling about it in your mind. Do you know what held me back from going after it? Me. I held my own progress back because I procrastinated for years. I kept putting it off and putting it off. And do you know I had the audacity to blame others for my lack of action? I blamed people from the church I attended. I felt as though they were selfish. I thought one of them should have taken me out driving and teach me what to do so I could get my license. But the truth was that I was a grown man, able to call a driver's instructor and get the lessons I needed for myself. I simply dragged my feet and kept postponing what I should have taken immediate action on.

When we get to the place where we are willing to take one hundred percent responsibility for our decisions and the results or lack thereof, we will really get somewhere in life. But if we keep blaming people or things for our own laziness in relation to our goals and dreams, we will find ourselves getting nowhere, year after year. No one who constantly plays the blame game excels in life.

I urge you to learn to be a person of action. You will get much further in your goals. In the previous chapter I spoke of a multi-millionaire who gave a few pointers and insights to me and a few of my fellow-workers. And I shared one of his words of wisdom with you which was about focus.

Another one of his insightful sayings was concerning the importance of taking action. He told us, "You cannot just think and grow rich."

I understood what he meant. Yes, thinking is a major part in the process. But action, and I might add, repeated and continuous action, is what will get you where you need to go. You can sit back and think all day. But until you act nothing will happen.

It is time to arise and pursue your goals. It is time to drop off the fear and intimidation which may be shouting at you, taunting you and telling you if you try you will fail. The greatest failure is to never try. Suppose you succeed? You owe it to yourself to at least attempt to fulfill your dream. Perhaps many others may benefit when your goals become a reality as well. So give it your best shot. Go for it.

People who master procrastination in life always rise to the top and excel in their pursuits. This is because, as they go after their goals, the necessary people and things come closer and closer to them. Actually, they are heading nearer to their destiny and so the two meet.

I love reading the Bible, and one of the greatest stories you will ever read is concerning Joshua and his mandate to lead the children of Israel into the Promised Land. It is found in Joshua chapter one. Moses had died and the children of Israel were in mourning for a while. Then the Almighty God spoke to Joshua and began his conversation with him by instructing him not to procrastinate, but arise and lead the people into their inheritance. God says in essence, "Moses my servant is dead, so arise and go over this Jordan." God was telling him, Moses is dead. You have mourned long enough. Now get over it and get moving. WOW, what a tremendous lesson to learn.

What are you mourning over? What are you living in regret for? Some things are over. Some things are done. Get over them and make up your mind to pursue your God-ordained destiny with renewed focus and energy. Perhaps you tried to pursue your dreams before, but things did not work out. Try again, and then again. Be bold and courageous. Be determined and relentless. Take action now. Seize the moment. Busy yourself in the pursuit of your goals and dreams. The time is now. So make now count.

Successful people master procrastination. That is why they win in life.

Chapter Seven
Diligence is Key to All Accomplishments

Diligence is the key issue to any worthy accomplishment. It is not a side issue. It is the key issue.

To be diligent means to give constant, careful, steady effort to a goal or task. It means to apply yourself consistently to something that you deem important to you. What you may see as important to you, however, may not be what others hold important to them. So, it is wisdom to never allow yourself to get bitter because someone does not believe in or support your dream.

I have met and been around talented people all my life. I well remember two young ladies who sang in a church service I attended. These women sang wonderfully. There is no doubt in my mind that had they known how and stuck with it their singing could have gone around the world blessing people. But talent alone is never enough to make a person successful. Everyone has at least one talent, one gift from the Creator. But some of the most talented people in the world are regrettably also some of the most laid back and, I dare say, lazy people in the world.

If you dare to arise and ascend into your purpose, you will experience more and more success, for persistent action in the right thing always produces rewards. But you will have to become consistent. You will have to make time for what is important to you. You will have to be diligent to do it, not once or twice, or when you get that special feeling, but constantly.

If you are going to reach your life's goals, you will have to apply yourself diligently to those goals step by step. Stop procrastinating, and stop it now.

You have been waiting to write that book for how long now? You have been waiting on the right time to produce that Gospel album for how long now? You have been waiting for this or that for how long now? When will waiting time be over for you to begin and persist in applying yourself to get what you could have gotten long ago, if you had only taken action and done so consistently?

When will it be time for you to rise to the occasion and pursue that for which you were created, that Divine purpose for which you were born? You may respond, "But I am waiting on the perfect time." My question to that is, **"When will you know it's the perfect time?"** If you are looking for conditions to be perfect before you diligently pursue your goals, then you may never fulfill them, for conditions may never be perfect.

If the truth be known, people who achieve noteworthy accomplishments will tell you that they succeeded because they acted on their dreams even when conditions did not look favorable. Conditions don't make the person. The wise soul with faith and action alters the conditions.

We are not where we are in life because of the conditions of our lives. We are where we are because we refuse to plan, set workable goals to fulfill that plan, and then take consistent and massive action towards our dreams. Dare to say, "I refuse for the conditions to remain this way, and with God's help, things are going to change." This is the attitude that wins. Dare to move in the direction of your goals, now.

Permit the wisdom God gave to King Solomon to bring this point home for you.

Ecclesiastes 11:4 (AMP)
"He who observes the wind [and waits for all conditions to be favorable] will not sow, and he who regards the clouds will not reap."

So don't wait for things to be perfect. Stop making excuses. Get moving. Be. Do. Have.

Successful people are diligent in their pursuits. That is why they win in life.

Chapter Eight
Diligence is an Action Word

Diligence is an action word. It is not a passive word. It is something we do, not something we just mentally assent to.

Diligence means that we attend to a particular goal or project refusing to be distracted by anyone or anything. In other words, when we are diligent, we are focused and steady in our pursuit. We have a target to reach, and we will do what it takes to reach it, regardless of the cost. This is diligence.

The Bible is, in my opinion, the greatest source of inspiration and motivation in the world. Make it a point to read it daily and it will change your life. Therefore, I would like to use the great example of a diligent man found in the Scriptures. It concerns a man of God, a prophet named Daniel, who is referred to as, "having an excellent spirit." **(Daniel 6:3)**

Daniel was diligent when it came to prayer. The principle of diligence works the same in any arena of life, whether it be spiritual, mental, social, business, finance or physical. With Daniel, it was of a spiritual nature. He sought God three times daily. He refused to let anything or anyone interfere with his time alone with God. To him, prayer was important. He did not just seek God when trouble kicked up as many of us do today. He prayed consistently. I mean, all the time. And while we may be specifically speaking of his diligence to prayer, keep in mind (as I said previously) that the principle of diligence and consistency works in any noble undertaking.

As I said before, Daniel was regarded as one who had an excellent spirit. He did things right. He did them because they were right. And he did them right, always going the right way rather than the easy way.

When you are committed to doing what is right and pursuing your dreams and goals in an ethical and proper fashion, it may seem at times like it is the hard way to go. But if you persist, refusing to back down, give up or quit, you will one day enjoy the sweet taste of victory.

Daniel's prayer life was the key to his place and power with God. Who do you know, whom, if they asked God, would get a supernatural revelation of another person's dream, not just the interpretation, but a revealing of the actual dream itself, so that he was able to declare the dream back to the king who demanded it?

This man walked with God and there is no denying it. One might state, God revealed things to him because he was a prophet." But read that particular happening carefully and you will see that God responded to Daniel because he prayed. I wonder what God would reveal to many of us in our respective places in the body of Christ if only we will spend much time with Him in prayer?

Daniel guarded his time with God in prayer. He refused to be distracted. Even when some leaders of the nation of Babylon, in which he was a stranger as a Jew, who hated him, and attempted to destroy him by deceiving the king into signing a decree that if any prayed to any other God other than the king himself, that person was to be thrown into a den of lions, Daniel, knowing that it was law, still went and prayed to the true and living Jehovah God three times daily as he always did.

What was going on did not matter to him. What other people did was not a deterrent to what he obligated himself to do. He was going to pray and seek God daily regardless of the cost. Disliking him did not matter. Working against him did not matter. Being in danger of being thrown to the lions did not matter. This is such an important lesson concerning diligence and its place in our lives.

When we are truly diligent about something, it would not matter what others think, say or do. Our focus is to get done what we have committed ourselves to. Really, a diligent person is a committed person. Commitment is not just a word. "I commit myself," is not just a phrase. It is not just the right thing to say in a wedding ceremony without any regard for what would happen in the future. This is why the divorce rate through-out the world and the church is so high. We do not understand the power of true commitment.

We think of it as just a word. But real commitment actually means that you stand for something and stay with it regardless of what others think or don't think or do or don't do. Diligence is commitment in action.

Daniel was so sold out to seeking God's Face that when he needed something from God's Hand the Lord graciously gave it to him. Prayer was a part of his life. It was a part of his daily schedule and he was committed to praying, period. Knowing they were plotting against him, he still prayed. Oh, we can learn so much from the life and actions of this anointed man of God.

Because Daniel stayed in the Face of God, seeking God even when being challenged by his adversaries, God saw to it that he was safe and delivered. God sent an angel from Heaven to take care of His servant, His friend. This mighty miracle affected the entire Babylonian kingdom. And Daniel's enemies, who were Babylonians, became the king's enemies as well. They were taken and thrown into the very same den of lions that they got Daniel thrown into. However, God's angel did not protect them. They were destroyed.

I used this example to show you how diligence always pays off in the end. If something is important and of great value to you then you should be willing to pursue that path and give it your all. If your God-given dream and your goals are vital to you, then you need to be diligent to do what it necessary, so that you can realize your potential and your true purpose.

35

Are we really committed? Do our actions line up? Are we diligent?

Successful people in every sphere of life are diligent in their goals. That is why they win in life.

Chapter Nine
More About the Power of Focus

Focus is diligence in action.

You will never meet a diligent person who is not focused and has his or her mind set upon reaching their target regardless of what they have to do. (Inside the realm of doing what is right). I love sitting and speaking with people who are focused. I enjoy reading stories about diligent people, especially those whose diligence has paid off and given them their heart's desire and a standing that no one can erase or take away.

If you and I are going to develop the trait of being diligent, we will have to ask ourselves some tough questions and answer them with the knowledge that we are in the mode or process of making life-altering decisions, choices which we dare not deter from regardless of how we feel. Our decisions and the way that we answer these questions cannot be based upon how we are feeling at the moment. **Feelings change. Decisions of quality do not.**

These questions are for the purpose of developing focus in our souls. No one gets far without being focused. This explains why most people do not get far in the pursuit of their dreams. You cannot win in the so-called game of life without focus. You cannot grow and develop without focus. You cannot be an anointed minister of the Gospel without focus. You cannot really enjoy success without embracing and developing focus in your life. And you definitely will not fulfill your goals and dreams without becoming and remaining focused upon them.

God gave us a mind so that we could focus. I remember an incident in the Bible where God Himself had to stop some people who were so focused and determined to do something contrary to His Will, that, had He not stopped them, they would have achieved their objective. God Himself said so. Read about it in Genesis chapter eleven. Focus is powerful.

I would now like to get into the practical nature of focus and how to develop focus in your life. It is really not that hard, but let me be up-front with you when I say it is disciplined.

The dictionary says that to focus means, "to center." It also means, "the center of attention." In other words, when you focus upon something or someone, you give it or them your undivided attention. Isn't that interesting? It reminds me of when a young man, or old for that matter, is deeply in love with a lady. As they speak, he focuses upon her every word. These lovers gaze into each other's eyes. They refuse to allow anything to distract them from each other. At moments like these, everything is on hold. She has his undivided attention. This is focus.

So when we become focused upon achieving a specific goal or purpose, we will give it our undivided attention. We will set our minds on reaching our target and everything else will have to wait. As an author of many books, I can assure you that this is very possible.

You must ask yourself what you really want in life. Take some time to think things through. Go where you can be alone somewhere and on purpose get still enough to listen to your heart. Pray and look within to discover your core purpose, what you were born to do or become. Shut your mind to idle thoughts and to the seeming conditions of life which may attempt to alter your destiny. Again, the conditions you are facing now have very little to do with what you can achieve and where you can go if you become a determined and focused soul. Over-comers overcome because they jumped hurdles, broke through barriers, slew giant situations and overcame challenges. So, what you may be facing right now may be just the thing you need to focus on and conquer to get to the next level in life.

One thing is sure. If you are going to win in life you cannot be afraid of obstacles. They will come.

When it comes to book writing, some people stand in amazement and wonder how I was able to accomplish what I have done in such a short space of time. I was even asked by various people to meet with them and share how I did it. The answer is simply that I know this is within my heart to do. I love writing. I enjoy sharing with others things I have learned that they also may learn, conquer and win. I believe that we all have the ability to rise to great heights and accomplish awesome things. And when God is in the picture the sky is not even the limit to what can be attained. You just cannot lose if you allow the Lord Jesus to direct your way.

Now book writing is what is in my heart. You need to set some time aside to determine what you are supposed to accomplish in life. Everyone has a purpose, yes even you. (Smile).

This is what you must focus on accomplishing.

So, get still and quiet your mind. Ask yourself, "What am I here for? What do I want to do with my life? What is my God-given dream? What are my goals and objectives?" If you do not have the answers to these questions, how can you focus properly for their attainment?

Set workable goals down on paper or on your ipad or kindle - whatever you use. Write them down so you can give your attention to them. Even the Almighty God had His intentions, purpose and will, written down. Successful people plan. And God, being the best at this, has so planned ahead and already revealed the glorious future in such minute details, that it makes us eager to one day be with Him to experience its grandeur and magnificence.

Take this lesson from the Wisest One of all and plan your life. Write your dreams and goals down. Do you want to master procrastination? Then take a moment before you read any further, and begin writing now. This is taking action. We already spoke of writing down your dreams and goals. And a few of you may have taken the time already to do so. But I guarantee that some of you have not done so yet. You put it off saying you will get to it when you have finished the book. And most likely, if you are like me, you may not get to it then either. So the only way that I know to get things done is to begin working on them immediately and get them done as soon as possible.

Remember, as someone has said so eloquently, "Success is not an accident, and neither is failure." Success comes by applying the right principles at the right time in the right way. Failure is refusing to take the needed actions which guarantee success. If you want to achieve success, then look at what successful people do, not necessarily the occupation they choose, nor their behavior and character, but the principles they live by and apply those wholesome principles to your life and chosen course, and you will win.

What do successful people do? They are diligent. They focus on what they want to accomplish and refuse to let anyone or anything deter them. That is why they win in life.

Chapter Ten
Diligence Based on Commitment, Not Feelings

Commitment is a word that is loosely used. Real commitment actually yields results because it is not based upon feelings. Feelings change, commitment does not.

There are many books that speak of the secrets of success, when in reality, there are no secrets. The reason they are held as secrets is because many people do not understand them or know about them. But the basic keys to succeeding and prospering in any given venture are the same as they have always been. And, believe it or not, they can all be found in the pages of the Holy Bible.

God, Who is the most successful Person in existence, revealed these keys throughout His Word and they are there for all who truly desire to learn them. Some people have written books on or about them, sharing their experiences from applying the keys, all revealing that these keys work for whosoever will. After all, God is interested in everyone becoming a winner in their given calling and profession. You need to realize and remember that. God is not against you being successful. Actually, if we follow Him closely, seeking His wisdom and applying the keys of success written in His Word, we are guaranteed to make our mark and accomplish great things beyond our imagination. God is for us, not against us.

One of the greatest keys to success is learning to be committed to a given task - so committed that you are determined to reach your objective regardless of the costs. You will pursue. You will persevere. You will keep on keeping on, refusing to quit until you realize your goals and dreams. This is true commitment.

Anyone who has accomplished anything worthwhile will tell you that this was the major key which insured his or her success. They simply were committed to the task. They stuck with it, refusing to see failure as an option. They were determined, persistent, diligent.

It did not matter how they felt. They pushed passed negative feelings. They refused to let how they felt determine what they would and would not do towards their goals and objectives. Until you come to the place where you can master your emotions, you will never amount to much in your pursuits. This is such an important point in developing a disciplined and diligent life that I would like to say it again. Until you learn to master and control your feelings, and not the other way around, you will never accomplish much.

Your commitment to your goals should be made based upon the level of the importance of each individual goal to you. In other words, you need to evaluate and determine the place each goal holds in your heart and life and then make your plans for the attainment of each, asking God each step of the way to lead you, guide you to the right places and people, and give you His wisdom to plan right and reach your destination. Whatever you do, please do not leave God out. You and I need Him. Because He created us He is the only One Who knows how much we can accomplish and He is very willing to help us. One of my favorite passages of Scripture is found in the Book of Proverbs. It will come in really handy for you as your pursue your goals.

Proverbs 3: 5-6
"Trust in the LORD with all thine heart; and lean not unto thine own understanding. In all thy ways acknowledge him, and he shall direct thy paths."

Your commitments to anyone and any venture should never be based on your feelings, but rather upon your commitment to your commitments. In other words, you should purpose in your heart that you will see each worthy goal through and that you will not stop until you have attained your dreams. You may have to change or tweak your plans here and there, but stay with your commitments.

Successful people are committed people. They literally hold fast to what they have set out to accomplish and determine in their hearts that they will not be stopped or hindered from reaching their target. Show me the person who always leans upon their feelings and I will show you someone who never hits the mark. Feelings change. They go up and down. Commitment on the other hand is stable and firm.

Our priorities can become distorted so quickly if we do not keep the main thing the main thing.

We need to evaluate our commitments. To be committed to a cause means to be sold out to it, to be dedicated and consecrated. In other words, our commitment is our focus and we will allow ourselves to be deterred. This is a must in this day and time. **So learn what it truly means to stand for something and stick with it. This is the practice of successful people.**

Chapter Eleven
Diligent People Think Differently

Proverbs 21:5
"The thoughts of the diligent tend only to plenteousness; but of every one that is hasty only to want."

Successful people think differently from unsuccessful people. Both have minds. Both have the ability to reason, imagine and dream. But while unsuccessful people always think in the light of the problems they face, successful people are solution driven. They think in terms of solutions and answers.

I have a good friend whom I have known for years. He was instrumental some time ago in getting me employed where he works as manager. My friend is very purpose-driven. He is a solution thinker. I remember going to him after encountering a problem at the job. I was bent on showing him who caused the problem. He was bent, however, on fixing the problem without getting personal. **"WOW."** It stopped me dead in my tracks. He was not interested in name calling or blame. He thought differently.

He looked at the same situation I was looking at, but with a different attitude towards it. I was thinking it was this person's fault. He was thinking, "Okay, what can be done to remedy this." And because he was thinking that way, he came up with the solution which fixed the problem within a matter of a few seconds. I was blown away. And I realized at that point I needed to change the way I was thinking.

Many of us look at the conditions our lives are in and throw blame on other people who, we feel, are responsible for where we are in life. We may blame our parents, grandparents, society, the government, some terrible boss we had, or God. Some of us even think that it is fate that is causing us to be unsuccessful in life. The truth of the matter is that we can change things in our lives whenever we are not pleased with the results we are getting. Think about it.

A person may say, "Oh, I do not have the job I want because I lack sufficient education." The solution is simple. Go back to school. Then again, the person may think, "But I am too old now." If your dream means that much to you, age should not matter. I do not want to go on and on with the excuses we come up with to defend our right to be lazy, laid back and unfocused, but suffice it to say, there is no excuse for making excuses. We are or can become whatever we decide if we are willing to take one hundred percent responsibility for our lives and choices.

The way we think has much to do with the results we receive. Even the Scriptures teach that as a person thinks in his heart, so is he. **(Proverbs 23:7)**

So our thoughts do matter. However, it is not just thinking that gets results. It is how we think which separates those who win in life from those who fail. This is what I learned from my friend. Just watching how he thought showed me that people think differently. If we learn to think of ways and strategies to better our situations, instead of thinking that we are stuck in our condition forever, it would make a world of difference.

Do not let your mind think like this: "Oh my God, I can't ever get out of this." Refuse to allow your mind to think, "Maybe this is my lot in life. I will never be any better off than I am right now. I am the product of my environment." Instead, learn to think like this: "What can I do ethically to change my condition? How can I fix this?" And, by the way, prayer helps greatly in this regard.

I find that many people do not like to use the mind the Creator gave them and think things through. We just follow the crowd, most of whom do not know how to think properly either. I am both amazed and saddened by the state of many of our young people today. It seems as if they have no focus, no true purpose for their lives. They just go from day to day, watching and following their friends who do not know where they are going either, living aimlessly, thinking that pleasure is all they need to live for.

We have not developed ourselves in the realm of thought. We focus more on now than we do on later. Then we wonder later why we are not successful, why, amidst our jobs or the lack thereof, we are not happy, fulfilled or satisfied. Permit me to go a little further even though I may ruffle a few feathers when I say, we take drugs now without thinking of the consequences later. We drink alcohol without thinking of the damage it may do to our liver later. People commit adultery now without thinking about the consequences later.

We are destroying ourselves and when some thinking person rises up and tries to show us what is going to happen later and why we need to change, we tell them that they are only trying to stop us from having fun. But what good is fun now if it will bring dire consequences later?

Truly successful people determine to live by principles rather than by feelings. They do not just think for now. They determine to see how their decisions now will result later because they are bent on building a dynasty and leaving a legacy for those who come behind. Listen. You can decide to have all the pleasure you want now, and suffer later, or you can determine to become responsible for your actions now and later be able to enjoy yourself to the max. A friend of mine said to me, "You can play now and pay later or pay now and play later."

Stop blaming others for where you are in life and make a firm decision that you will become a solution thinker and think your way out of your condition.

I would encourage you to invest in your mind. Get some good books on the areas which interest you and read them. If you want to succeed, find books on success and feed on them. If you desire to be a doctor then read along those lines. Make it a point to feed your mind with as much information as you can about the areas you desire to excel in. Knowledge gives the capacity for change. It creates the possibility for transformation. So it is vital to gain understanding, feeding your soul with more and more information until you are literally thinking different. A different way of thinking will produce different actions which will result in different results in your life.

Our minds operate by knowledge which is fed to it. So, if it is constantly hearing and feeding upon positive things, it will bring forth positive results. Feed the mind. Do it on purpose. Do not allow just anybody to dump things in your mind, without examining them in the light of truth, to ensure that your mind thinks right and properly.

Also, remember that knowledge alone is not enough. Apply the good wholesome information to your life. Nothing happens without action. So, as you gain knowledge, and push your mind to think positively, do what you read. Do not procrastinate. Act and act now. If you see that it is good, godly and proper to work and save, do so. Refuse to be idle. Refuse to hang with friends who see labor as slavery. Work is a good thing, and can prove to be a great source of joy and fulfillment, if you discover your God-given purpose and pursue that as your work.

Thinking differently will result in living differently. So if you do not like how you are living, change your thoughts and you will change your life.

Successful people dare to think differently. That is why they win in life.

Chapter Twelve
Diligent People Refuse to be Lazy

Laziness is never the trait of the diligent soul. The opposite of diligence is laziness.

According to **Webster's Thesaurus,** synonyms of the word diligent are: **"active, assiduous, bustling, employed, engaged, industrious, laborious, occupied, sedulous, tied-up, working."**

The word, "assiduous" means, (according to Webster's Dictionary), **"to be marked by careful unremitting attention or persistent application."** In other words, to be diligent involves much focus. Compare what you have just read to how Webster's Dictionary now describes what it means to be lazy. The word lazy means, "not easily aroused to action or work."

Its synonyms are, and I quote, **"idle, indolent, shiftless, slothful."** Related words, according to Webster's Dictionary are, **"apathetic, drowsy, dull, inert, languorous, lazyish, lethargic, listless, quiescent, sleepy, sluggish."**

I know some of those definitions may have stung a little. However, they do describe the manner in which some of us conduct our lives don't they. Laziness and diligence do not go together. They are opposites.

In contrasting the diligent person with the lazy, take a look at these ten facts written in the Book of Proverbs, the Book of Wisdom:

1. The hand of a diligent man or woman will never spend all the money they receive. They will always save something. This is an important key to enjoying financial security. Stop spending all you have. Save

something. Place it in a bank or a bond account where it will get interest and work for you. On the other hand, lazy people always spend what they get, if they get anything, thinking that they cannot afford to save. Please realize this important fact: If you choose pleasure over responsibility, you will always regret it. But if you choose responsibility over pleasure, the day will come when you can have all the pleasure you want without the regret.

Proverbs 10:4 (AMP)
"He becomes poor who works with a slack and idle hand, but the hand of the diligent makes rich."

2. The diligent man is not afraid of work. He or she works with the gifts God has given him or her, while the lazy man hangs around vain or worthless people. The old adage, "Birds of a feather flock together," is found to be true many times. People who truly want to get somewhere in life and in God do not hang around those who are not interested in pursuing their true purpose. (Proverbs 13:20)

Proverbs 12:11
"He that tilleth his land shall be satisfied with bread: but he that followeth vain persons is void of understanding."

3. A lazy person will always lack. This is because lazy people always want the reward without putting in the work. They dream about being successful. They dream about it all day long. But they refuse to wake up and apply themselves to make their dreams a reality. So, they desire all day long, but never realize the fulfillment of their goals. On the other hand, diligent people prosper.

Proverbs 13:4
"The soul of the sluggard desireth, and hath

nothing, but the soul of the diligent shall be
made fat."

4. Diligent people are thinking people. But not only are
they thinkers, they are doers. A very focused business
man, known for his focus, said to me, "You cannot
just think and instantly become rich." I got his point.
It is good thoughts applied which get results. The
similarity of the diligent and the lazy is that they both
think. The difference between the two is that one
stays thinking only and talking only, while the other
applies himself in order to reach his destination.

> Proverbs 21:5
> "The thoughts of the diligent tend only to
> plenteousness; but of every one that is hasty only to
> want."

5. Lazy people want pleasure without responsibility. On
the other hand, diligent people choose responsibility
over pleasure, knowing that if they place
responsibility over pleasure the day will come when
they will have all of the things they desire.

> Proverbs 12:27
> "The slothful man roasteth not that which he took in
> hunting: but the substance of a diligent man is
> precious."

6. Diligent people will always hold great positions in
life and will rule. Lazy people will always have to be
led and ruled by forced labor.

> Proverbs 12:24
> "The hand of the diligent will rule, but the
> slothful will be put to forced labor."

7. Diligent people, because of their focus, will always
be sought out by other diligent people.

Proverbs 22:29
"Seest thou a man diligent in his business? he shall stand before kings; he shall not stand before mean men."

8. Diligent people have no problem with work. Their goals and dreams mean much to them. So they will push to accomplish their purpose. On the other hand the lazy man has opportunities available to him, but refuses to take them. They simply do not want to work hard, to do what it takes to make things happen for themselves. Everyone has gifts, talents and abilities given to them by Almighty God, which, if developed properly and used, can provide the person with more than enough to take care of himself and his family. Lazy people do not want to take the time to train and develop and better themselves. So, they end up with nothing.

Proverbs 24: 30-34
"I went by the field of the slothful, and by the vineyard of the man void of understanding; And, lo, it was all grown over with thorns, and nettles had covered the face thereof, and the stone wall thereof was broken down. Then I saw, and considered it well: I looked upon it, and received instruction. Yet a little sleep, a little slumber, a little folding of the hands to sleep: So shall thy poverty come as one that travelleth; and thy want as an armed man."

9. One of the most interesting ways to describe a lazy person is found in the Book of Proverbs. There, God says that a lazy man can listen to seven different people telling him why he should work, and he would give them, in his opinion, a valid reason why he should not. Lazy people are full of excuses. Regardless of how you attempt to push a lazy person to accomplish something of worth and value, he or

she is too busy to listen to you. They are busy doing nothing, but making excuses. This is why a diligent person reaches their goals while the lazy can only day-dream about it.

Proverbs 26: 13-16
"The slothful man saith, There is a lion in the way; a lion is in the streets. As the door turneth upon his hinges, so doth the slothful upon his bed. The slothful hideth his hand in his bosom; it grieveth him to bring it again to his mouth. The sluggard is wiser in his own conceit than seven men that can render a reason."

10. A diligent person watches over what he or she has. They are not wasteful. They do not waste what comes into their hand. Yes, they count even their pennies. They are meticulous. They are planners. They do not just deal with now. They look ahead. This is why I said that they never spend all their money. They save something because they always stay focused upon their goals. One of the greatest examples of a diligent man found in the Old Testament is Joseph. He was extremely focused and determined in his pursuit to ensure that people were able to be fed during the famine that was coming. He saved twenty percent of all the food of Egypt. It is absolutely interesting to note that people who have acquired much wealth and riches encourage us to save at least twenty percent of our income. (I wonder where they got that.) God taught Joseph that principle, and by applying it, he saved many lives. Joseph was a diligent man. May we follow his example and enjoy the results.

Proverbs 27: 23-27
"Be thou diligent to know the state of thy flocks, and look well to thy herds. For riches are not for ever: and doth the crown endure to every generation? The hay appeareth, and the tender grass sheweth itself, and herbs of the mountains are gathered. The lambs are

for thy clothing, and the goats are the price of the field. And thou shalt have goats' milk enough for thy food, for the food of thy household, and for the maintenance for thy maidens."

I trust that these ten facts will inspire and motivate you to move daily in the direction of your dreams and goals. Remember nothing happens without bold, consistent, persistent, determined massive action. So take action now.

Successful people refuse to be laid back and lazy. That is why they win in life.

Chapter Thirteen
Diligence Involves Persistence

The key of persistence and perseverance is vital if you desire to be successful in any endeavor. Many of us simply give up too soon.

We give up right before our breakthrough comes. It is true that it is not easy to keep on keeping on when things are looking contrary and everyone is saying that what you are attempting to accomplish is not working. Yet amidst all of the distractions and challenges which attempt to deter us from our course and focus, it should be noted that those who develop stick-ability usually get much more than what they were after. Persistence is usually the actual key which opens the doors of favor and success when nothing else seems to work. It has proven to be the difference between winning and losing for those who have a passion and deep desire to see their goals become a reality. No one gets to the finish line without it. According to the thesaurus, to be persistent simply means, "to be continual, unrelenting, constant, determined and pushy." In the context of which we speak, it implies staying with your goals, pursuing them with a focus and relentlessness that will not accept defeat or give up, until that desire is attained. In other words, be diligent to go after your dreams.

When we make up our minds that we will have something that is worthwhile, not breaching the laws and principles of God, nor bringing hurt and damage to our fellow-men, after gaining the knowledge necessary for the achievement of our dreams, putting pen to paper devising a workable plan of action which can be implemented immediately, all that is then needed is the mastering of procrastination and the elbow grease of work, which recognizes no such thing as defeat, refusing to quit until we get to that place called done.

This is being proven all over the world. People are applying the key of diligence, which is persistence, to the attaining of their goals, and they are winning in life. It does not matter what is going on in the world. When you are determined and persistent, you can accomplish your dreams.

Have faith in God. And believe in yourself. Believe that He has given you the ability to make something of your life. Believe in the talents and abilities He has bestowed upon you. Ask Him to show you the path to better living, to reveal to you a purpose for your life upon which you can set your focus. An idea or ideas, an impulse, a dream will come to you. Seize them. Put pen to paper and map out a strategy. Make that plan do-able. Create one that is so workable that you can begin to implement it immediately. Realize that with God, nothing is impossible. And if you persevere you will find that your breakthrough and BIG MOMENT will come, maybe right as you reach what you think is going to be the end and result in failure. If you are willing to stay with your goals and dreams, working on them daily, you will be amazed at what all can be accomplished.

I am not kidding when I say that you will experience challenges. You may have set-backs. People, well-meaning but misguided people, may encourage you to give up. Giant obstacles will come in your path. But perseverance can win over them all. The true winner never quits.

PRINCIPLES WORK FOR WHOSOEVER WILL WORK THEM. This is so true about the key of persistence. So do not quit or cave in.

At times you may have to tweak your plans. You may have to chart another way to your destination. You may even have to make some revisions here and there. But do not give up on your dream. If the desire within your heart to realize your goals will prove to be of benefit, not just for your personal welfare, but also the welfare of your family and others as well, then it is worth your time and attention. Let this become your focus. You are not just persisting for you, but for your family, your friends, and others who need what you have to offer. So stay in the game.

If you will pray; if you will stay; if you remain strong; if you sing a song; if you run and if you keep on keeping on; if you do right and stick to your pursuit day and night, one day, somehow, someway, you will see, the things you fought for will come to be.

Successful people are diligent and focused. They devote their time and attention to their dreams and goals. This is why they win in life.

Chapter Fourteen
Diligent People Develop Winning Habits

Our habits can take us to great heights or bring us down to the ground, all depending upon what we practice on a daily and on-going basis.

One of the most difficult things for people to embrace is that if you are going to learn to be successful you may have to adopt new attitudes, habits and behaviors. Our past attitudes and patterns of behaviors are what has us in the conditions we are in today. If we do not like the results we are having we will have to change our habits so that we can experience different results in our lives. You cannot expect to realize success and victory with a mind-set of failure and low self-esteem.

Someone has said that to do the same things you have always done, expecting to get different results is actually bordering on insanity. You cannot plant oranges and expect to see apples. Likewise, our patterns of behaviors have us where we are right now. In order for us to transform our lives we will have to change the habits we have for the more empowering ones which guarantee our success. People who win in life, accomplishing their dreams and goals have developed habits over a period of time which caused them to be where they are today. Many of us want the results they get without learning and adopting the habits they developed over time to get where they are.

I firmly believe that each of us are in this earth for a purpose. We are here to do something, be something worthwhile and make a positive difference in this world. The Creator knew we were coming and devised a plan just for us. The key to success is to find out what that purpose is and walk it out one day at a time, one step at a time. This will require new attitudes, focus and behaviors, for much of what belongs to us will not come our way if are not prepared for it.

Each of us can be successful. Yes, even you.

In order to do this, we will have to do what is necessary to make our dreams a reality. Forming and developing the right kinds of habits is important if we are going to get things done and experience the sweetness of a dream fulfilled.

For example, I spoke before of a multi-millionaire who shared with a few of his workers, including me, concerning three keys to being successful in your life, regardless of who you are or where you were born. I already shared two of his insights with you. The last one he gave to us was the importance of reading books. He is not the only successful person I heard say that either. But suppose you are not a person who likes reading. You will have to be willing to change this attitude and be willing to develop a new habit.

In order for something to become a habit, you must do it over and over again, until it locks in and begins to be like second nature to you. In other words, we will have to practice something by choice, not feelings, until our bodies are trained in it. Then we will actually find ourselves doing it because it has become something we do. In other words, you must become diligent at it.

Diligence, as we have already stated, is a constant, steady effort and focus to accomplish a goal. It is constantly working at something, until we have arrived at our desired destination. So, if I do not like to read, but I decide that I must develop the habit of reading in my life, then I must set aside time to read each and every day.

If I start to read a book, and continue to do so day by day, at some point I will finish the book. If I continue to read other books, remaining steady and determined to finish, one day, I will find that I have developed a habit of reading. Usually, when I share with people how to develop the habit of finishing a book that they have started, I say to them, "Keep reading and at some point you will finish." You see, I love reading. It is a habit that I have developed in my life through constant effort, through diligence.

The ability to begin a project and stay with it to completion is diligence in action. When we give ourselves to something (whether good or evil) on a consistent basis, we develop a habit. Someone said that if you practice something every day for six weeks or more, you would develop a habit of doing whatever you practice. Another person said that we are creatures of habit. I believe that these statements are both true. Anything that you give yourself to continually will become habitual. So if you don't want something negative to become, or remain a habit, then don't practice it.

Our habits are the direct result of our practices or what we do daily. This can be a positive thing or a negative, all again depending on what we are practicing. Really, the law of sowing and reaping is always in operation and yet many of us think that life is so unfair. This principle does not only apply to finances. It includes each area of our lives. What we as individuals sow, we will reap. So if you practice the wrong kinds of habits, they will become your reality, and so will their rewards or consequences. Think about that and ponder it carefully. If you do not want to see the fruit of some negative thing manifested in your life, do not engage in and practice habits which lead to that result.

I used an example similar to this before, but please permit me to use a personal example or two from my life to get this point across. I needed desperately to lose some weight. I was told by a very reputable weight loss company that I was really overweight. I was also told this by a dear friend, who took a risk in telling me, thinking that it may have hurt our friendship. But I have learned that true friends will praise you when you are right, but also tell you when you are wrong. Faithful are the wounds of a true friend. So, I did not get upset. I knew my friend was telling me the truth.

Knowing I needed to lose weight, however, was not enough for the weight to drop off. It remained. I also found out from this reputable Weight-loss Company how many pounds I needed to lose and the fact that I was going to have to change my eating habits. But I learned quickly that information alone never did anything to help a person lose weight. It was important. It was necessary to get this knowledge. But knowledge that is not applied will not profit any one.

Please do not misunderstand me at all. Get the information you need to change your life. Read books. Listen to experts and successful people who have experiential knowledge. This is half the battle. You have to know before you can do.

So please be hungry for information which can be helpful to the attaining of your dreams. But if you do not do anything with what you learn you will not be the better.

When I got the knowledge of what to do I was pumped up and ready to go. I was ready to change my eating habits. But I do believe that particular motivation ended before the evening was up. My old habits did not want to die easily. They encouraged, urged and even pushed me into eating a fast food that completely went against my diet. So, my mind reasoned that I should begin the next day. The following morning, and I might add, on many occasions, it was a different story. My flesh and mind stood in firm agreement that I should begin the next day and the next day and the next day. Procrastination will destroy you, your dreams and goals, if you keep adhering to it.

As it pertains to exercise, the same thing happened. Oh, I started to do some exercising. But, when the pains and aches began, it was another story. Yet I had set a goal. I wanted to lose unnecessary weight. I desired to get the excess pounds off and feel better. However, I now needed to develop some new habits which would enforce my victory and breakthrough. This is where so many of us have failed. We have desires. We have dreams and goals. We have written them down. And we are sitting idly by, waiting for our proverbial ship to come in, so that we can set sail comfortably. Howbeit, the ship rarely comes in. It stays out there, where we can see it, urging us to swim to it and take charge of our lives and destiny. You can have goals and dream idly all day long. Until you are willing to pay the price and do what is necessary to get where you are longing to be with your family relationships, finances, weight, walk with God, education, business or any other chosen field of endeavor, you will not get there. And the habits you attain by daily practice will determine how far you go.

As it pertains to this matter of weight loss, I am on my way. What causes success? Much of the time it is the willingness to change. We must decide to alter our behaviors and actions to get what we desire from and in life. What produces change? The willingness to develop the habits necessary to get where we desire to go.

I desperately needed to develop the habit of drinking more water. This again was going to require focus and diligence. Discipline was going to have to be the name of the game, for I rarely drank water. I would go for days without drinking it. I drank soda and other beverages. So when it was made clear that I needed to drink water every day, I had to develop the habit of doing so, regardless of how I felt. (I may need to do an entire chapter in this book on pushing past your feelings, because it is vital to do so if you are going to attain your dreams and goals!)

I took action immediately and began to drink at least four cups of water daily. This in itself was a big achievement. Then I moved it up to six cups of water daily. I did this every day until it became a part of my daily routine. Now for the most part I drink at least seven or more cups of water daily. And I no longer drink soda like I used to. I may drink one in a month. But the strong desire I had for it is gone. I changed my habit. I did so as an act of my will, the Lord being my helper. I kept at it until the force of habit kicked it. In other words, when I began, I had to make myself drink water and stay away from soda. This, at times, was not easy. But as I kept on, it got easier and easier. Now, it is not even a battle for me anymore. It is now my habit to drink water.

This can be done in any realm of our existence. I just wanted to use this particular one to drive this point home. If you desire to be successful in your goals, you need to find out what changes you need to make in your behavior, attitude and actions and then determine, with God's help, to make those changes.

I would like to end this particular chapter by giving you a few ideas on how you can develop new and life-transforming habits which can assist you in achieving your dreams.

1. Realize that change is necessary to accomplish your goals.

2. Find good books and information concerning what it will take to reach your goals.

3. Begin immediately to implement the things which you learn. Refuse to Procrastinate.

4. Learn the power of persistence. Things may seem difficult when you begin to develop new habits. Just stay at it until the habit is fully formed. Then it will become normal for you.

5. Keep your mind on your goals, not on the necessary sacrifices you have to make to attain them. Remember that focus is important. What you focus on will become your reality. So constantly keep your mind on the end result.

Successful people know that they may have to develop new habits in order to get where they desire to go. That is why they win in life.

Chapter Fifteen
Diligent People Respect Time

The wisdom principle of respecting time is vital to success.
This is an important statement which should not be ignored.
Each of us are given the same amount of time, twenty-four
hours in a day. What sets apart those who succeed from those
who fail is how each individual uses the time allotted. How
you and I value and use our time, will decide how far we go
with our goals and dreams. In this area of success, the greatest
enemy to time that we will have to face and defeat is a thing
called procrastination. The habit of postponing and
continually putting things off keeps most people from
reaching their true God-given potential.

The reason why procrastination is such a great enemy is
because if you keep putting off doing the things which lead to
your goals, you will never attain them. Those who continually
say, "One day I will get to it," usually never get even close to
their target. You must learn to work with time.

While the Creator gave us time for our benefit, time can prove
to be a great friend, or your worst enemy, all depending upon
your respect for it or the lack thereof. And you should also
consider the fact that people who attract success in their lives
on a consistent basis are those who are very time-conscious.
After having the pleasure of being around some very
influential people in various stratus of society, it is very
important and noteworthy to state that diligent people regard
time as precious. They guard their time with full awareness
that what they do with the time allotted to them will
determine the kinds of results they receive in life.

Truly successful people have no problem sharing with others
what they had to do and what they learned on their way to
where they are. But they do have an issue with those who
have no regard for the value of time. They do not believe in

wasting time. They, of course, enjoy life. They have their moments for leisure and pleasure. But to a person attempting to reach new places of achievement, time is held as sacred. And if they determine that a person is not interested in understanding principles which can lead to winning in life, they would not share the glorious truths which have made the difference in their lives.

What are you doing with the time given to you?

On a few occasions I have spoken at our fellowship here in beautiful Nassau, Bahamas and shared with them the reality that we each have twenty-four hours in a given day. Eight hours can be used for sleep. Another eight hours can be used for work (when you are working for someone else). You still have eight hours left. And even if you use four or six of those to spend with family (which is vital), you can still use two hours to work on your dreams and goals. Do not let your precious gift of time just slip through your fingers. Use your time wisely.

Here are some facts about time which may prove to be helpful:

1. God has given each of us the same amount of time. In this regard, all of us are equal. We each have been given twenty-four hours. If we use eight hours to work on someone else's job, and eight hours to sleep, we still have eight more hours. We can use between two to four of those hours to write a book, work on a song, read books which can help us to advance in life, draw closer to God, etc.

2. Decide how to use your time wisely. Wasting time is not a good thing. Putting off things which can be accomplished if we give attention to them will prove to work against you if procrastinating continually becomes a habit. So do your best to make your time count and work on your goals.

3. Be diligent to protect your time from those dream thieves who would attempt to lure you away from doing the things which are productive and crucial to your success. This is one trait of the highly successful which many have not yet comprehended. Guard your time. Do not do it at the expense of your family or your times of relaxation. But learn to set dates to achieve your goals, and get to them with persistent and consistent action. The time you spend on them will determine how close you get to them. Value your time. Successful people have a healthy respect for time. This is what has placed them in the successful position they enjoy. Learn to follow in their steps.

We have stated this again and again in this book, but it bears repeating, for it is the hallmark of champions. Refuse to procrastinate. Take control over your time. Get busy pursuing your goals and dreams. Set your time-lines and ensure that you meet those deadlines.

Successful people are diligent at using their time wisely. That is why they win in life.

Chapter Sixteen
Diligent People Master Fear

Fear has stopped more people from becoming successful than any other evil thing.

God Himself is against fear, and continually encourages us in the Bible to, "fear not." Fear paralyzes and causes those who cower under it to dread the unknown. Fear carries with it a terrible thing called terror. This off-spring of fear produces worry and anxiety, which can develop over time until those held in its grip have problems sleeping, eating or taking action on their goals.

Being afraid of failure is one of the root causes of procrastination and this cannot be denied. What holds people back from singing that song, writing that book, taking that new job, beginning a business, or even flying on an airplane? Fear. I have found that people hold themselves back in life because they are too afraid to take action. They think, "Suppose I attempt to do that and fail?" Their minds are consumed with images of failure and regret.

I am going to first of all show you the folly of fear, and then will attempt to show you how to get rid of your fears and seize your destiny with courage, determination and faith. You are not in this earth to be a failure. Defeat is not your name. You can win in the realm of life if you are willing to practice some principles which will alter the way you look at things.

I have spoken about my situation regarding how long it took for me to take my driver's test so that I could receive my license. Now I would like to share with you why I waited so long before I took the test. I was afraid so I procrastinated for years. Therefore I got my license at age thirty, instead of age eighteen when I could have gotten it.

"But of were you afraid," you may ask? The answer is even more strange, for I allowed the fear of hitting an inanimate object to keep me from my goal of being a licensed driver. In my country when we take a driver's test we are required to go and park safely between two plastic cones, without hitting them, and then to come out from the cones without hitting them. The reason that I hesitated to take the test (for years I remind you) was because I was afraid of hitting the cones.

Now, it is noteworthy that many people hit those cones and fail the driving exam. However, it is also a fact that many people take the test and pass without a problem. It all depended upon your preparation. I could have had my license years before I got it if only I had enlisted the help of a Driving Instructor, several of whom could be found within the pages of the phone book. Instead of doing that, I procrastinated and prayed for God, somehow, someway to help me get my license.

If you do not believe that fear will cause you to do foolish, useless things, you had better think again. Common sense dictated that I go and take driving lessons and then go and take the test. Fear, however, kept pointing out that if I took the test I might fail. Common sense revealed that my chance of passing the test was more apt to happen if I enlisted help. Fear still pointed out that I may fail the test so I had better not try until I was sure. I was letting something which had no substance, no reality, and no foundation hinder me from having what rightfully belonged to me.

Thank God for a brother who helped me out. I guess he got tired of seeing me without a car. He spoke with a Driving Instructor and after just two lessons with her, she signed me up to take my driving exam. I remembered that I had not seen her for a while and I called and asked her what happened. She responded, "You can drive. I have put in for your exam." I took the exam and passed it on the first attempt. I went between the cones and parked. Then I came out. WOW. I could have done it when I was eighteen. I could have done it when I was nineteen, twenty, twenty-one, twenty- two and on and on. But I allowed fear of failure to hinder me. I permitted fear to blind me to reality. I procrastinated because I was afraid. Therefore, I suffered needlessly always having to catch a ride. My family suffered needlessly. And it was not necessary at all.

What about you my friend? Are you allowing fear to stop you from reaching for your dream? Are you allowing fear of failure to hinder you from stepping out on your goals? Are you afraid of what people may think if you fail? Suppose you succeed? What will they think then? Are you scared that you may not have what it takes to get done what you need to get done? Maybe you do, maybe you don't. But how will you know if you do not try and keep on trying. You may just surprise yourself.

Fear is a master at intimidation. And if you let it intimidate you, you may never take action on your goals. Do not let it rule you. You can conquer your fears. You can realize your dreams. "How?" you ask. Simply by taking bold and determined steps toward your goals. Just do it. Write down what you need to do to get where you desire to go, and then get the knowledge and information necessary to get there. Then go for it and keep going for it, regardless of how you feel. When you have won some victories and seen that fear had no basis or foundation, you will determine not to let it master you again.

Here are three passages from the Bible which I have found extremely helpful through the years. They will encourage you, inspire you, and motivate you if you think about them and mutter them to yourself over and over again. Here is the first one;

Joshua 1: 8-9
"This book of the law shall not depart out of thy mouth; but thou shalt meditate therein day and night, that thou mayest observe to do according to all that is written therein: for then thou shalt make thy way prosperous, and then thou shalt have good success. Have not I commanded

thee? Be strong and of a good courage; be not afraid, neither be thou dismayed: for the LORD thy God is with thee whithersoever thou goest."

Let that passage of Scripture speak to you. It will motivate you to take bold massive action and realize the dreams in your heart. Here is the second passage;

Isaiah 41:10 (The Amplified Bible)
"Fear not [there is nothing to fear], for I am with you; do not look around you in terror and be dismayed, for I am your God. I will strengthen and harden you to difficulties, yes, I will help you; yes, I will hold you up and retain you with My [victorious] right hand of rightness and justice."

When you know God has your back and that He is for your success, it makes all the difference in the world. You are not alone. He is there to help you win in life. So you have no need to fear as you take persistent action on your goals.
Here is the final passage;

Philippians 4:13
"I can do all things through Christ which strengthens me."

Wow. That says I can. I can do all things through Christ which gives me the strength to do the things I need to do. So, I can fulfill my goals and dreams. I can overcome the hurdles I face. And I can burst through fears and make some things happen. I can walk in my God-ordained destiny one step at a time, one day at a time. I can. I can. I can. And so can you.

Successful people are diligent to conquer their fears, refusing to allow anything to hold them back from pursuing their goals and dreams. That is why they win in life.

Chapter Seventeen
Diligent People Are Relentless

Perhaps one of the most interesting definitions of the word diligent is relentless.

This word describes the very essence of what diligence is all about because it captures our attention and makes us unyielding, insistent, ruthless, obstinate and uncompromising. It really denotes a person who will not quit or give up regardless of the hard times and circumstances with which they are faced.

I like this word particularly because of its warlike connotation. It describes a warrior who refuses to be defeated. This is the attitude which wins. If you are going to attain anything worthwhile you will have to make up your mind that you are in for the long-haul. You will not give up, back down or fall away. You will reach your goals and that is a settled matter as far as you are concerned.

I wish to create in your mind an attitude of victory. You are not a loser and it is time for you to rise up and be all you are destined to be. You have what it takes to fulfill your God-ordained destiny. You can make it. You can become what you are envisioning in your heart. All it takes is an obstinate and uncompromising stand that refuses to accept defeat. No one gets far without this kind of thinking. You must pursue. You must persist. You must overcome.

Relentlessness is shown by successful people in every arena of life. When you are desperate enough and desire something strongly enough that you are prepared to pay the price of pursuing it until you get it, you will develop the winning attitude becoming relentless. This is a powerful force which refuses to know anything except victory. Winners win because they won't quit.

I would encourage you to read the autobiographies and biographies of great men and women who accomplished outstanding feats and see how relentless, unyielding and even obstinate they became in pursuing their goals. Their passion for the dream pushed them to the extent that they were unwilling to let go of it. Some may have even lost friendships along the way because the other party did not believe in their dream, and attempted to stop them from going after it. To say that fighting for your cause would not cost you something is ludicrous. It may cost you friendships which you need to lose to get where you desire to go. It may cost you giving up habits you enjoy to develop new ones you need to get to your destiny. It may cost you some of your leisure time so that you can use that time getting further educated for the task ahead. But if the dream is worth that much to you, then pay the price and reap the reward.

As we said before, one of the definitions of relentless is to be obstinate. This word has some interesting definitions which may drive home the point I am attempting to make. The word obstinate means, "to be stubborn." (I am using this term in a positive sense. We are not speaking of being stubborn in a wrong thing, a wrong behavior or habit. We are speaking of refusing to give up on your goals and dreams.)

The word obstinate also means, "Determined, fixed, unmoved, tenacious, headstrong and adamant." Now I know you get the picture. **People who get somewhere in life purpose to get there.** They do so regardless of the contrary circumstances. They defy the odds. They stay away from the nay-sayers. They make things happen.

If you are going to follow in their steps you will have to have the tenacity of a bulldog. You will have to be prepared to stand and stand strong against opposition. There is just no getting past the fact that you will go through challenges. But the greater the battle, the sweeter the victory if you are ready to fight for what you believe in. And you must believe in your God-given dreams and your goals in order to see them become a reality.

Can you become steadfast? Can you push and press your way through? Sure you can. You can do more than you realize. It is absolutely amazing how our minds work. For instance, how many of us know that much of the fast food we consume is not good for us? Yet we eat it and some of us must admit that we do this daily. What a waste of money and focus. (I am not saying that you should refrain from fast food. Just stick with me a moment for I am trying to make a point.)

Now, I am attempting to show from a different angle how our minds work. If you are like me you may have been told you needed to lose a few or many pounds. Maybe you were told that you were grossly overweight. I hope you did not get offended, especially if you know it is the truth.

So, let us suppose for the purpose of this lesson that we are told such things by our family members or friends. We then make a half-hearted decision that we will adhere to the advice and shed a few pounds. We declare our intentions. But by the evening of the same day, or maybe the next, we are right back to our old habit of eating wrong.

After attempting to do this on occasions, even exercising a few times, we finally call it quits, thinking we can never change. Our bodies got used to this habit and it seems so hard to stop eating the stuff which puts the excess fat on us. Then, one day we have a problem with our hearts, or some other part of the body. The problem, according to our doctor, is related to the excess weight we are carrying. And we are told, "If you want to live, you will have to exercise daily and stop eating certain foods now. This is not optional. Either you begin this now or else." What happens in your mind, the same mind which told you that you could not change? It immediately begins to help you to change because your life is at stake.

Alright, let us apply that to everything we do. What are the downsides to not reaching for your dreams and goals? Do you want life to continue as it is for you? Are you happy and satisfied? Or are you miserable knowing you desire better things for your family, yourself, for your relationship with the Lord Jesus, for others?

Things will not change until you make the firm, no turning around decision to change and relentlessly pursue your purpose. To believe something else simply means you are living under a delusion. Maybe you are like I was in that you just think perhaps one day things will get better. "I just have to hold on until my time comes." The truth is that our time is here, now. You and I only have a certain length of time to be here on earth. Then we are out of here. So let's get busy now pursuing our God-ordained purpose. It is up to us to determine what we desire and then to formulate goals with God's help to make those things a reality. I believe that if we trust God, He will give us ideas, concepts and insights which if applied with persistence and consistency, can transform our lives for the better.

You can see your dreams come to pass. You can experience the joy of a purpose fulfilled. You will have to be very focused and head strong and stick with your plans. If you know they are good, right and noble, and if they are not contrary to God's Word, and they will not hurt and negatively impact others, then you have the right and the God-given power to pursue them relentlessly.

Successful people are relentless in their goals. That is why they win in life.

Chapter Eighteen
Why People Fail

I believe that the seeds of greatness are in every individual on the face of the earth. Yes, this includes you too.

We each have the capacity to accomplish great things and the potential to excel. The Creator of the Universe has made all of us, and He has given us gifts, talents and abilities which can impact our lives, as well as the lives of others, for the better, if only we will embrace what we have and learn how to use them wisely.

For some reason many people believe that success is automatic. They think that if you are successful you were born to be that way and if you are a failure fate has designed you to be that as well. This is simply not true. You are here to win in life. You are on this earth to make a difference. You count. Your value is far above what you may even fathom. If only you would actually be still and ask the Lord to show you the meaning of life and what part you can play in it. Ask Him for an idea that will completely revolutionize your life and the lives of other people as well.

As it pertains to success and failure, the reality is that there are reasons why people fail in pursuit of their dreams and goals. Things do not just happen. There are always those actions or inactions which precede the events and we are in control of the results we get if we learn how to diligently persevere. Nothing is impossible if we believe enough to act and keep on applying ourselves towards our true purpose.

As I sit here writing I am thinking of so many who show great ability, but seem to be stuck in some kind of rut and procrastinative behavior pattern which is in essence causing them not to experience all they can be, do and have. We have so much going for us. It is actually both very humbling and yet very empowering to realize how much faith God has in us, that He has invested so many talents and abilities within us that we might do great things.

Let us take a quick look at seven of the reasons why people fail to obtain their dreams and goals. Maybe you can see what is possibly holding you back and how you can get past it. We are doing this particular exercise, not so you could beat yourself up for what you have not yet accomplished, but so that you can possibly identify those dream thieves which can hinder your progress if you permit it. Here are seven major causes of unfulfilled goals and dreams:

1. Failure to reach our dreams can be because we have no dreams. That is simple enough, right? What is your dream? Do you have a vision for your life, your family, your finances, your career, your health, etc? You need a dream for each area of your life. If you do not know your purpose, set some time to get by yourself and think things through. Ask the Lord to help you and ensure that you have a plan for your life.

2. People fail because they do not break their dreams down into goals and objectives. You need to have workable steps which you can begin to implement immediately. Write them down and keep them before you. What are you plans for this year? Are they written down? Make sure your action steps are do-able.

3. One of the greatest causes of failure is that many people procrastinate. They pull back from acting on their goals. Without action nothing is put into effect. Once you have broken down your dream into workable steps which you can begin to do right away, take action on them. If your plans are not broken down simple enough for you to begin acting on right away, then you have not thought them through enough. Again, make them do-able.

4. Failure happens because we give up too soon. Consistency is the key to breakthrough. If you really desire to succeed, you will have to learn to be consistent as you pursue your goals and dreams. Never, ever give up. Stay at it. Keep on keeping on.

5. Failure happens because of a negative mind-set. Our thoughts have power. And how we think will affect how we speak and how we behave. So it is important to develop the mind-set of a winner and think nothing but victory. Remember, as a man thinks in his heart, so is he. How can we develop the mind-set of a winner? That is discussed in another chapter of this book. So read on.

6. Failure can be the result, and much of the time is the result, of broken focus. This means that we begin applying ourselves to our goals and seem to be doing pretty well. Then distractions of various sorts come and we get side-tracked and derailed, If this is your situation, it is not too late to begin again. Get back up and get going on your goals with a determination that you will not become unfocused anymore.

7. Some people fail because they have not yet discovered the awesome power of saying, "No." That's right, it is a good thing to say no at the right times. When it comes to our goals and dreams, we will have to learn to say no at various times to distractions. These may come in the form of people and other things, some things being in themselves alright, but we simply do not have time for them if we are to complete our goals in the timeline that we have set. One of the greatest causes of failure in this regard is, again, a lack of focus. So guard your time and learn to say no when necessary.

We do not have to fail when it comes to attaining our goals and noteworthy dreams. And even if we have stopped pursuing them for some reason or another, we can regain our focus and get back to achieving our purpose. So, if you have allowed other things to distract you for a while, do not beat yourself over the head about it. Just set your mind once again in the direction you want to go and dream again, believe again, pursue again and you will find yourself, with God's help, reaching your goals moment by moment. Remember that successful people reach their goals, not because they never fail, but because they never quit. They see the failures as lessons in themselves. They learn from their seeming mistakes. And they allow those lessons to guide them in the future so that they do not meet the same fate again. Learn from them.

Winners never quit. They diligently pursue their purpose. That is why they win in life.

Chapter Nineteen
Diligent People Develop A Winning Attitude

People who diligently pursue their goals and dreams with focus, determination and persistence have a winning attitude. They refuse to think failure. They literally set and settle it in their minds that they are going to plan their work, work their plan, and by God's grace they will succeed. This is how they think and, therefore, they are not moved when things don't appear to be working in their favor. They simply persevere and persist and push past all resistance until they hit their mark.

This is a trait present in all true achievers, regardless of their pursuit. No one can be successful who does not alter their thoughts and decide to think win-win. To believe you can be successful with a negative attitude is self-delusion.

Think like a failure and it will surely hold you captive like a prisoner.

One of the greatest attributes you can ever develop is that of a winner's attitude and mindset. How we think in regard to life is of the utmost importance. Our thoughts, and in particular how we think about ourselves, about God, other people and things will be the determining factor in how we live and how we deal with the issues which confront us on an on-going basis.

Let us for a moment look at the mind in relation to realizing our goals and dreams. We are told in the Bible that as a person thinks in his heart so is he. In other words, our dominant thoughts will be become our reality. We will live our lives, make our decisions and thereby attract things and people into or dispel them from us based upon our attitudes and mindset. How we think determines how we speak and the choices we make. If our attitude toward life is negative, we will constantly speak negatively and make decisions which are not in our best interest. The results we experience will be based upon what we think and believe in our hearts. But if we choose to keep a positive mindset, and be consistent in speaking positively, regardless of external circumstances, we will make better decisions and reap the rewards of those choices.

But how do we develop a winning and positive attitude? I am so glad you asked. I can speak from experience because I once was very negative, and had to fight to gain a positive mindset. It was not easy to do. But I persevered and was able to accomplish it by the grace of God to the extent that I am now thinking more positively, and experiencing greater results and having more peace and stability in my mind.

When I speak of thinking in a positive manner I am attempting to impress upon you the importance of thinking right thoughts so that you can speak right things, exhibit right behavior and experience better results than you may be having right now. Our thoughts play a key role in our success or failure. We live our lives based upon our most dominant thoughts. Attitudes do matter.

I was not always a positive thinker. I know that some may think I am speaking of mind over matter. However, I am more conveying the truth that as a person thinks they become for out of our hearts comes the issues of life. For many years, I lived in a state of depression because it just seemed as if I could not get things to work in my favor. I tried to do the right things. I was hoping for the best. But inwardly I was a wreck going somewhere to have a wreck. I did not realize I was causing many of my own problems because of my negative attitudes toward life. Even though I was trying to change my conditions in various areas of my life, my mind was not set strongly in the purpose of God. I was not settled in my soul that it was the will of God, and my rights as His child to prosper and live out my dreams and goals. I was actually a prisoner to my circumstances, not because I could not get out of the prison, but because I did not realize that the doors were open and I could walk out any time I wanted to.

I thought wrong. I thought of myself as a failure. And I lived like one too. I tried, prayed, hoped and cried. I wondered if I was destined to fail. At least these kinds of thoughts tried to persist in my thinking. Have you ever been there?

Here is how I rose above them. I began to develop a new attitude about life. I read my Bible and I read other books, and begin to change the information which seemed to dominate my thoughts. I made myself think positively. I pushed myself to keep an attitude of gratitude and an attitude of winning. I was not born to fail. It was not God's plan for me to be a loser. I was created by Him to accomplish great things. All I had to do was believe.

My attitude changed when I altered my way of thinking and began to keep a more positive view of life. And yours will too. New information will result in new ways of thinking, which will result in new attitudes. You must learn how to think like a winner and set your mind on reaching your goals before you can believe you are able to achieve them.

How important is the right attitude in regard to accomplishing our dreams? The answer is, "Very important." We have to think right in order to get right results. This is such an essential area that I would like to go further in showing you the power of your thoughts.

We actually live our lives by our most dominant thoughts. We speak and behave based upon how we think and what we think on most of the day. So if we are thinking that we can never accomplish our goals, we will believe that we cannot do so, and the result will be continuous procrastination.

This is why people keep putting things off over and over again. We are afraid that we may fail. Our attitude toward that particular goal is one of failing because thoughts of failure dominate our minds. To stop this we must put positive information in - information which tells us that our goals and dreams are possible. We will have to, for a lack of better words, load and bombard our minds with good, wholesome and powerful information which can cause our thinking to shift from negative to positive, from an attitude of thinking failure to one of success.

There are so many good books to read and audios and videos to listen to from good and respectable coaches which can help in the transformation of your mind from a negative mindset to a positive one. And if you want to change the way you think or learn how to develop the habits which will guarantee your success in any given field, I mean if you really desire change, then you should avail yourself to these. I had to really work at altering my mind because I had conditioned it negatively for a long, long time. It took work to change it. It took effort. It took a lot of reading and it took continual casting down of the negative thoughts which constantly seemed to bombard my thinking. It took diligence.

But, with God's help, I got it done. I persisted. I read material which showed me the proper mindset to have. I read, most of all, my Bible. I listened to people who had learned to do this before me and therefore transformed their lives. And I am telling you that thinking right makes a tremendous difference in the results we receive in life. So, to develop a proper attitude for winning in life, we must learn to think positively.

I would encourage you to also watch the company you keep in this regard. We will look at how the people you hang around continually do matter in another chapter, but suffice it to say, much of the time, the attitudes we display are largely affected by the company we keep. Sayings such as, "You are known by your friends", and "Birds of a feather flock together," is true much of the time.

So if you determine that your goals and dreams mean that much to you, look closely at the people you hang around and ask yourself if they are a positive influence on your life, or a negative influence on your life. Be honest with yourself. This does not mean you will have to stop being friends with some if you see they have a negative effect upon you and the way you think and behave. Depending on the depth of the influence, you may have to loose them and find new friends. Then again, it may mean that you simply have to distance yourself somewhat from them until you can develop a positive mindset, and then aim to influence them to be more like you instead.

"Does attitude really matter when it comes to reaching your goals and dreams," you may ask again? Absolutely. Let me show you how:

First, the right attitude will give you hope. When you think that it is possible to attain your dreams, you will find yourself constantly thinking about them. Your mind will keep looking for ways that they can be attained.

Second, having a positive attitude will cause your enthusiasm to run high. It's called an adrenaline rush. You will want to use this enthusiastic spirit to help push you more and more in the direction of your goals. Take it from me that this pure high which comes from knowing that attaining your goal is possible can get you far in your pursuits. This is one reason why the company you keep is important. You do not want anyone around you talking negatively about your dream, taking your adrenaline away.

Third, when you have a positive mindset of where you want to go, it just makes your goals and dreams that more do-able.

I can sense that some who are reading these words have lost their enthusiasm for the dreams they have in their hearts. Maybe something did not work out the way you thought it should have. Maybe you have struggled to make your vision for your life come to pass and it yielded little or no results. Or perhaps, after the experiences you have had, you just cannot see how it is possible for you to reach your goals.

If any of these things are your plight, I am encouraging you to rise up once more, remember your God-given dreams, and begin to believe once more that those dreams are possible. Dare to dream again. Dare to imagine yourself being that person, accomplishing that goal, finishing what you have started. Plan again. Maybe your plans were not as doable as you needed them to be. Get back at it. Pray. Imagine. Dream, Believe.

Successful people win in life because they are diligent to develop a positive mindset. They choose to believe things are possible, even when others say otherwise. That is why they accomplish such great feats. Do what they do. Work at developing the right attitudes in life, yes, a positive attitude. It will astound you how it will transform your life for the better.

Chapter Twenty
Purpose, Dreams & Goals

The wisdom principle of planning is vital to true success and achievement. The Book of Proverbs, mostly written by one whose accomplishments speak volumes, (so that we need not doubt the accuracy of his advice), teaches that we should plan our steps, and ensure that they are done with God's guidance and wisdom. Planning ensures that we are able to focus upon a worthy goal or dream and remain focused until the completion of the same. Planning is right at the beginning stage of all noteworthy accomplishments.

First, we need to have a dream - that is, a vision for our lives. Then we need to develop a vision plan, also known as goals, as to how we will reach the fulfillment of our dreams one step at a time. The greater the vision, the more elaborate the goals and steps should be to reaching our God-ordained mark.

Planning, as some professionals are quick to point out, can prove to be time consuming and mentally exhausting. This is because planning involves thinking, reasoning and being strategic. If we are going to be successful at anything, we need a plan.

Solomon reveals that it is up to us to devise a plan, and let God direct our steps particularly when it comes to things we would like to achieve for ourselves, our families and our generations to come.

Some plans are short-term, meaning that with due diligence and focus, we can accomplish them in a short frame of time. Others may take years of work and persistence to see them realized. But if the plans are valuable to you, then you should keep at them until you accomplish them. There is much that can be said about the advantages of planning and how to plan. But here are just a few suggestions:

Ensure that you know what you want out of life. What do you want to do? What do you want to attain? What do you desire to experience and enjoy in life? What is your God-given dream? What vision stirs within your spirit consistently, and what do you dream about all the time? Is it wholesome, decent, godly and possible? Then begin making plans to be that, do that, have that. And begin making those plans now. Refuse to procrastinate. Begin right away.

Ensure that your plans are not beyond your reach to begin to implement right away. In other words, make your plans doable. Set them in such a way that you can start putting your plans into action right away. There is a reason for this. When plans are made in such a manner that they overwhelm you, your energy gets drained just thinking about them. You will find yourself wanting to avoid beginning at all costs and with a whole lot of excuses. Making the plans workable from the get-go ensures that you stay pumped up and ready for action.

Write your plans down. This is such an important point. Even the Sacred Scriptures admonished a prophet of God to, "Write the vision and make it plain upon tables, that he may run that reads it." (Habakkuk 2:2, The Holy Bible) Writing your plans will help to ensure that you remain focused upon your goals. What you write, you can remember, because you can always go back and look it at. Focused people reach their goals, because they refuse to be distracted. They keep their plans before them, day and night.

Do you really want to be successful? Do you want to win in life? Then do what the winners do. Get a vision for your life. Make your plans. And keep them before you.

Chapter Twenty One
A Notable Lesson in Goal Attainment

I have been, through various lessons, attempting to show you that your goals are achievable if you are willing to take bold, persistent, and consistent action toward them. And regardless of how I worded each chapter, if you look closely, you will realize that there is one common thread on every page. It is this particular idea upon which I desire that we set our minds, until the reality of it dawns upon us, pushing us forward in bold and aggressive action that refuses to be deterred, distracted or derailed.

If you understand what I am about to say, then you will comprehend what I have been saying all along, and it will change your life. It will give you a new zeal for living, a perception that you are capable of far more than you have ever dreamed, and that you are the only one standing in the way of reaching your God-given destiny.

By now I believe I have gotten your attention. Your curiosity is at an all time high and you are clinging to every word as you read so that you dare not miss the idea, the point to which I am alluding. This is not a secret as such, for it has been discovered by every successful person in every generation, and from every walk of life, whether it be spiritual, mental, emotional, physical, financial, or even in good, lasting and enjoyable relationships.

Those who have applied this principle spiritually have drawn closer to God on purpose, just because they wanted to, and enjoy such a sweet place in Him that many envy their status. They literally walk with Him and carry His power and people can recognize that there is a marked difference between this person and others with whom they associate.

Those who apply the principle mentally astound us with the magnitude of the development of their minds and what they know. To them, the issues which puzzle the masses are no issues. They look through and think through every problem and come up with solutions which are so simple, that those who fret over and worry about the problems stand in awe as they hear wisdom pour from the lips of these kinds of people.

I know what I am speaking about. I have a dear friend who, in such humility and grace, baffles me, and I am sure the same happens with others when they get around him, at how simple solutions to seemingly complex issues come to him. Actually, I know of several people, not many but few, who are solution oriented rather than problem oriented. They have developed the habit of thinking things through. And because of this, Fortune Five Hundred Companies and beyond search out individuals of this nature and hire them to do that very thing. My friend of whom I speak is one of such rare people. Did I say, "rare?" Yes I did. Why do I say that, you may ask? The answer is because most people prefer to let others do all of their thinking for them.

The principle that I refer to has made successes in each arena of life, because it is a principle. It is a rule. It does not change. And once you determine to live by it, it will make you a winner regardless of where you are right now, or your condition in life at the moment.

"Please tell me. What is this principle, this life transforming principle of which you speak?" I can hear you asking. Believe me that when it is revealed, you will think, "But I already know that." And while that may be true, it can never be truly known until you literally live by it when it comes to the attaining of your goals. You most likely have applied the principle numerous times. When you did, it worked for you. Perhaps you have not realized that the principle works for everything, not just some things. Most of the time when you applied the principle you had no choice. You had to do it. And it worked. What most people have missed, however, is the reality that the very same principle can be put into

87

practice, without waiting on life to push you into using it. You can apply it just because you want to, in order to ensure that you get where you desire to go.

I would like to tell you that fear is the one thing which keeps people from applying the principle. And winners in life, in every strata of society, have won because they determined in their own hearts not to allow fear to master them any longer. After all, the feelings of fear may seem real, but usually the reason for the fear has no basis of truth. In most cases fear is unfounded. And yet many allow themselves to be paralyzed by it. Are you one of them?

Oh, I can hear some pleading with me, "Please do not get distracted. Please tell me the principle of which you speak with which I can reach my goals and dreams, changing my life and bringing to me the things I desire." The answer is simple. Are you ready? Are you on the edge of your seat? Do you really want to know? Then here it is:

"TAKE REPEATED, CONSISTENT, AND AGGRESSIVE ACTION STEPS DAILY TOWARD YOUR GOALS AND DREAMS WITH DETERMINED FOCUS AND THE MINDSET YOU WILL NOT CAVE IN, GIVE UP OR QUIT UNTIL YOU GET WHAT YOU ARE AFTER."

"But," you say, "I already know that. That is nothing new. I know." But then again, if you are not applying the principle of consistent and persistent action, then you really don't know, do you?

Chapter Twenty Two
Diligent People Puts First Things First

Active investigation of successful people has made me aware of the fact that they have mastered the art of prioritizing their lives on the basis of what is more important to them, line upon line.

They have learned how to make and keep the main thing, the main thing. Success is relative, that is, what may be classified as success to one, may not necessarily be success to another. This is why being critical and judgmental is unwise. I once heard someone imply that if a person was not financially wealthy, they were not successful. I do not agree with this. I believe that anyone who desires to be successful financially can do so simply by applying the principles which guarantee financial accumulation. But money alone can never be classified as success because it is so limited.

What is money if you suffer from a disease which cannot be cured by medical science? This is why we must also set physical goals of believing God for healing and health and doing what we can to ensure we live healthy. Then again, money can never give you salvation and the awesome joy of knowing your sins are forgiven and you have the blissful hope of spending eternity in the magnificent Presence of the Most High God? People who attain wealth but do not know the Lord will find their money worthless when, not if, they pass from this life. You are not carrying your money with you. The only way to ensure that you go peacefully into the next life and enjoy God's presence forever is by asking Jesus Christ, the Son of God, to come into your heart as your Lord and Savior, believing He died for your sins, and arose, for you to be right with God. (I know some may not like this, but it is something to seriously consider, right? After all, where will you spend eternity? That should matter to you more than anything.)

Then again, am I belittling having money and saying that it is not a worthy pursuit? Not at all. I believe it is our right and God-given privilege to plan, set goals and attain success in every area of life, including finances. A careful, honest, and unbiased study of the Holy Bible will reveal that the Creator of Heaven and earth is all for our success. As a matter of fact, those who dared to walk with Him enjoyed experiencing His favor and blessing on whatever they set their hands to, because He created us to be winners in Him and in life.

Now, as I was saying, success in one individual's life may not necessarily be success in another's. This is because we desire different things. So never compare yourself with others. What is your dream? What are your goals? What is in your heart to do, to become, to have and enjoy? When you determine to understand your purpose for being and set your heart and mind to the pursuit of that consistently, you will find that being envious and jealous of others truly makes no sense. Your God-given destiny is calling you. Your dreams await you. So thank God for others and their pursuits, but focus on what you should be doing.

The only way you will keep the main thing the main thing and focus on first things first is if you are prepared in your mind to plan where you want to go and set deadlines on when you expect to attain what you are after. Then, get after it. Life is really that simple. Of course, there is work involved. No one can get something accomplished without getting it accomplished. So it will take effort and energy. But if it means that much to you, if you really want it, if you know it is your God-given right to have it, be it or do it, then get after it and do not let the circumstances or situations of life deter you from your goals.

I have read stories of those who attained incredible feats, remarkable things. Some have already passed on, while others are still living. There is not a single one of them who were not faced with adverse circumstances. As a matter of fact, most of them defied seemingly impossible odds to get where they needed or desired to go.

They pushed, struggled and persevered. Most of all, they kept their focus. They kept their dreams before them. They refused to be distracted. In other words, they kept the main thing, the main thing. This is the only way you and I will reach the goals and dreams we have in our hearts. We have God's help. And He will work with us all the way. However, we must stay focused.

To help you experience the truth of this statement, and the sweetness of a goal fulfilled, I would like for you to set a goal which can be accomplished. Something do-able. Then write it down. Also, write down how you intend to get where you want to go. In other words, make a workable plan of action that will help you reach your goal. Make it DO-ABLE. Make the plan so simple that you can begin to implement it right away. It may take you a hour or more to devise such a plan. Do it anyway. Ask God for His wisdom and help with your goal and plan.

Then get to work. Start doing the plan and stay focused. Make up your mind that you will see your plan through. It may cost you some of your television time. It may cost you some of your recreation time. But, if the goal, the dream, is worth that much to you, the sacrifice will prove to be well worth it.

I have already alluded to this fact, but right here, it bears repeating: You may have to say no to some things. Actually you will have to say no, if you want to reach your goals. But keep first things first.

Successful people are diligent to keep the main thing, the main thing. This is why they win in life.

Chapter Twenty Three
Learn From The Wise

Proverbs 13:20
"He that walketh with wise men shall be wise: but a companion of fools shall be destroyed."

Do you really desire to be a winner in life? Are there goals and dreams you want to see fulfilled? Then do yourself a favor and learn from those who have already accomplished great things.

Learning from others is not an easy thing for some people. This is true. Many people do not like being corrected. They do not like to be shown they were doing something wrong. For example, a person may go to someone with sound financial advice attempting to understand why they are having so many problems in this area. They may say that they need some advice. However, when the financial expert shows the person that they spend too much or that they made some poor financial decisions, the one with the issues, instead of embracing the advice, contends that they had to make those choices because of what was going on at the moment.

What is so interesting is some of the excuses given. You know, "I needed to go on vacation, so I had to borrow the money. After all, I needed break." Or, "I had to get the clothes because this was a SALE of a lifetime and it was going to be over the very day I run into it. If I did not use the credit cards right then to get all of the clothing I got, I would have missed the sale." What about, "I could not save any money. I don't have enough now to deal with all I have to deal with." A wise counselor, in order to destroy that myth, may ask, "Do you have money to go to the movies, or to buy fast food for lunch every day?"

Of course, this may result in another set of excuses being given, such as, "I need my times of recreation," etc. The real truth is that you will never get anywhere financially if you do not learn to put responsibility first and pleasure second. And people who are of substance will tell you, "If you learn to place responsibility first, the day will come when you can have an enjoy life. But if you put pleasure first, the time will come, and sometimes continually, when you will suffer painfully and by the way, needlessly."

I know from personal experience that if you and I are going to win in life and reach our goals, we will have to learn to hear correction and walk in the wisdom of those who have gone before us so that we know what it takes to get where we desire to go.

I am thinking about myself as related to a seeming weight problem I had. For years, people kept trying to tell me I needed to develop better eating habits and exercise daily. And the people who constantly spoke to me ranged from those in the Weight-loss Industry to well-meaning friends, who had a right to talk for it was obvious they were doing something right.

In reality, I did not have a weight problem. I had a food problem. This produced the weight situation.

I needed to change how I was eating, and that was a fact. I loved eating the greasy foods. And I drank mega sodas and drinks full of sugar. I said I wanted to lose the weight, but in reality I was deceiving myself. I was not prepared to change. When people spoke to me of my weight, and what I needed to do to alter my situation, I offered excuses. Again, correction does not come easy for some of us. But one thing is evident and that is, when you do not make the decisions you need to make, the decisions will be made for you. And that is a sad place to reach, for it is avoidable.

I would encourage you to read through the writings of Solomon in the Book of Proverbs and see what he says about the person who refuses correction. For one thing, he says that the person who refuses correction is a fool. **(See Proverbs 1:7)** Oh my.

I do not want to be a fool, do you? Well, if the old saying is true that, "Birds of a feather flock together," we would do well to ensure that the company we keep walks in wisdom in their daily affairs. "Who is a wise person?" you may ask. The answer is varied, but can be summed up in the following manner: A wise person is one who loves correction and is always willing and endeavoring to change when he or she realizes they are wrong.

A wise person is one who embraces correction, and that is why they get where they are. No one was born into this world perfect, other than the Lord Jesus Christ. Everyone has to learn. Some learn quicker than others, but we all have to learn. If you and I keep that in mind, we will learn to take correction better.

Our lives are the way they are because of decisions we have made. "Well," you may say, "I did not make a choice." Then you made a decision not to make a decision. Once you have reached a reasonable age you become the product of choices you make. And the only way to change the results you are having is to change your decisions.

This is a lesson wise people will attempt to teach us. Do you want to experience real change? Then make a change.

But who should you and I listen to may be the next obvious question, right? After all, we do not want to open our minds to just anybody. I believe there are various people placed in our path, whether in person or through their books, audios, videos or websites. These people have information and experience vital to our learning, growth, and development.

We may need different mentors because we need help in various areas of our lives. One may be able to help and advise us financially, but not able to mentor us in our marriage relationships. Then again, one may be able to help us when it comes to choosing good friends, while we may need another to teach us skills we have to learn to get to another level in our career.

Determine what you need and then search out those who possess the knowledge and wisdom concerning that area of life. If you desire spiritual help, find someone who knows the Holy Bible and can give you advice and insight from the Word, and who lives what he or she teaches. If you need to change your diet and eat better, exercise and gain control when it comes to your weight, do not look for one who eats poorly and never exercises. Make sure you find one with sufficient experience and who does things ethically.

There are those whom I get counsel from. Some I know or have met and then again others I do not know personally. I have learned their stories, however, and found their advice to be true if I apply myself to it. I encourage you to get some mentors in your life who can help you and give you good counsel to attain your goals and dreams. The right kind of people speaking into your life can make a tremendous difference.

Successful people are diligent to learn from others. That is why they win in life.

Chapter Twenty Four
Diligent People Are Disciplined People

Discipline is not a bad word.

It is of primary importance for those of us who desire to attain our goals. To be disciplined means, to train ourselves in something worthy and desirable. The dictionary says that to be disciplined means, "to be regimented," which means to be well-ordered, well-organized and closely controlled. Now I know you can join organizations which restrict and force people to be disciplined. But in the case of our lessons, we are speaking of disciplining yourself in order to work at and accomplish your dreams.

Will it take such a term to get where you are attempting to go? Surely it will. Diligence is a must to attain a purpose. And discipline is a part of being diligent. Remember our working definition of diligence: to give constant, careful, steady effort to a desired goal. This actually reveals the disciplined life. In order to give constant and steady effort to accomplish a dream, you and I have to train ourselves to do what we need to do consistently, until we attain our ideal.

This may entail us learning new habits, while at the same time dropping old ones that may be keeping us back. As a matter of fact, experts tell us that while developing the process of success, more will be happening within us rather than just externally. It is what the principles of success make us and how they improve us, thereby improving our situations and circumstances, that makes the big difference. The discipline needed to reach our goals trains us and establishes certain good habit, core values and practices in us which enable us to handle the responsibility of true success.

By the way, please stop saying that life is hard. It is not hard. It simply calls for discipline. Do not be afraid of that word, **"DISCIPLINE."**

Discipline is really your friend. And if we learn the principles which guarantee success in reaching our goals and dreams, we will taste the sweetness of dreams realized. I believe you are actually about to have some of the greatest times you have ever had. It is simply a matter of applying yourself and doing those things you need to do to get where you desire to go.

So, make up your mind to train, to discover new ways of doing things, new attitudes and new behaviors. Push yourself. Make up your mind to make your mind think the way you want it to. Yes, make your mind your servant. Ponder the path of life you want to experience and make sure you can live with not just your decisions, but the results they produce as well. And if you do not want the results, discipline yourself and quit doing those things which lead to those results. Every choice we make carries rewards or consequences. And the quicker we learn this, the sooner we can make better decisions.

I know this is a sore point to make, but I believe it will bring home what I am attempting to say. Everyone should know that smoking cigarettes is not good for the body, right? And yet many people, even some who try to teach their children not to do so, are going through two and three packs daily. Ask them, "Do you know this is not good for you?" They will answer, "Yes, I know."

"Then why are you doing it?" Some will respond, "Because it looks cool." (No it does not). Others may answer, "Well, it's a force of habit." Examine those words carefully and you will see that any person can kick any habit by the power of force of habit. And of course, if you depend on God like I do, His supernatural power can help you to break any addiction.

A habit is something you practice until it becomes second nature to you. In other words, a habit is the result of doing something over and over again, sometimes by force, until you start to like it and begin doing it without even really thinking about it. It becomes you. If bad habits are developed, then why can't we work at some new ones, better ones, which can work in our favor?

Now, as I was saying, people know smoking is not good for them. Even the companies which sell it have it on the box that it is not good for you. Yet people persist. Then one day they find out they have a terrible disease which can kill them. And they begin to really regret that they did not stop this habit before it ruined and destroyed their lives.

We understand this when it comes to smoking. But can we likewise understand that the reason our lives are in the shape they are in financially, physically, socially, and even spiritually, much of the time is because of habits we have practiced and participated in for years. The practice of spending when we should have saved; of speaking and being inconsiderate and unkind to our spouses; the continual eating of greasy and fatty food, refusal to exercise, and refusal to drink water; and many other vices we have practiced that may have gotten us where we are right now. Do not despair. I am not trying to discourage you. What I am attempting to show you is that if negative practices led to developing habits which have caused us problems, what will happen if we determine to discipline ourselves and learn new habits which can bring us success and victory in life? After all, life is not complicated. It is simply disciplined. You have to learn discipline.

Train yourself to finish projects you start. Train yourself to walk a particular distance at least three times weekly. Train yourself to eat better, to order a salad with your meal, or as your meal. Train yourself to drink less soda and more water. I know you may not like it, but do it until you do. Train yourself to attend church weekly, never giving yourself excuses why you should not go. Discipline yourself to get your driver's license, or to learn that new skill which can help you get where you want to go. Work on yourself. Read the books you need to read. Take the course you know is essential to reaching your dream. Do it, and begin now.

Truly successful people are that way because they have exercised the discipline of diligence. That is why they win in life.

Twenty Five
Diligent People are Steady

I am quite sure that most of us have heard that old story called, "The Tortoise and the Hare." I heard this story when I was just a little boy. It is a popular tale of how a tortoise beat a rabbit in a race. The rabbit, knowing it was faster than the tortoise, decided because he was so far ahead in the race, to take a break and rest. He fell asleep.

And while he slept, the tortoise, who was not fast, but was persistent and consistent, passed him by, winning the race.
The moral of the story is quite simple. Steadiness and persistence enable us to accomplish great things if we refuse to quit.

This is a trademark of the diligent soul. In order to accomplish your dreams and goals, you will have to learn how to remain steady in your pursuits, regardless of how things may appear. Understand that adversities will come. Hard times will show up. Struggles are a part of the journey. But the determined soul wins.

When we speak of being steady, we are referring to that wholesome trait of doing what you need to do consistently until you receive the results you desire. Mark well the person full of potential, but lacking the enthusiasm to keep going in the direction of his or her dreams. That person will never truly amount to anything until he or she learns how to be steadfast. "What is steadfastness?" one may ask. The answer has been referred to so many times throughout this book that you will laugh when you hear it. To be steadfast means, "to be unwavering, persistent, committed, dedicated, firm, unfaltering and resolute."

So a steady soul is one who is sold out to a cause, who is determined to reach a destination, one who is focused. This person knows what they want, believes it is worth undertaking, and refuses to quit or give up until they make their dream come true. If you really want to know what it means to be steadfast, let me use a definition which shows the negative side. It is the word, **"stubborn."** That's right. To be steadfast means to be stubborn, to be fixated upon an idea, ideal or purpose, refusing to let go of it regardless of who does not agree with it. In order to truly succeed at anything worthwhile, you must know when it is time to "draw the line in the sand," so to speak, and make up your mind that you will have the results you want and nothing is going to stop you. Of course we are speaking of good, wholesome and positive things, not things which are harmful to you or others.

If you want to reach your goals you must develop an attitude, a proper mindset that you are not a quitter. Quitting after things get difficult will not only stop you from attaining your desired purpose, but can impede any future success you should enjoy, because you can form a habit of backing off other endeavors whenever the going gets rough. So, you will have to become firm in your pursuits. People of substance are those who simply will not give up. That is actually the only difference between those who win and those who lose in life.

So, are you a quitter? Or will you develop the characteristic of steadfastness? If you truly desire to make something of yourself, to accomplish a worthy goal or to fulfill your God-given dreams, you will have to learn the power of staying with your purpose until you get what you are after.

Steadfastness is what makes winners out of normal and ordinary people. It will make a champion out of you as well.

Chapter Twenty Six
The Diligent Win

I know that you have probably read or heard most, if not all, of the various principles we have discussed in this book before. And that is fine because hearing these things over and over can result in a transforming effect if you grasp the understanding of them, and apply yourself to them.

What is so interesting is that, while many people may have learned about these principles, so few people experience their reality. The reason is obvious, even though many of us do not see it. We give up too quickly.

We would hear great speakers and motivators tell us what we need to do and inspire us with their speeches. Some of us paid good money to attend the meetings they held. Oh, we got motivated alright. We were ready to take that leap of faith, pursue our goals, and realize our dreams. However, after coming out of those workshops and seminars, many of us got back to our various places of abode and after attempting to apply what we learned for a period of time and maybe seeing little, if any results, we decided that what those speakers told us does not work.

The truth of the matter is that principles work, and they work for whosoever will apply them diligently. That's right. **The diligent win.**

You will never get where you desire to go without becoming determined and persistent in the pursuit of your goals. You must make the effort and the effort must be consistent. If this point I am sharing gets your attention, then it was well worth writing this book to inspire you.

I am an avid reader of books. I love it. Reading opens my thinking, inspires my intellect, and broadens my knowledge.

Learning what others know by experience helps me to gain from their successes, and also from their failures, if they are honest and share them. My favorite book of all is the "Holy Bible," which I firmly believe is the inspired Word of the Living God, for no mortal man could have penned such marvelous truths on his own. Let skeptics criticize me all they want, but by listening to and walking by the principles in the Scriptures my life has dramatically been transformed.

One of the great lessons the Bible teaches is the successes and failures of heroes of the faith. It does not cover up the flaws of people like King David or his son, King Solomon, who was blessed by the Almighty with so much wisdom that he was hailed as the wisest man who ever lived. Yet Solomon died as a fool for not heeding his own wisdom, a lesson from which we can all learn.

What about people like Daniel or Joseph? How about Moses and Joshua, and Caleb? What do these people teach us about winning in life? If you study their lives closely, you will discover that they won in life because they held fast to what God told them, refusing to quit or give up. They diligently pursued their God-ordained destiny and stayed with it in spite of the odds. Challenges came every step of the way. Much of the times things did not appear to be in their favor. Yet they persevered.

Oh, if you ever feel discouraged and need some inspiration - I mean some get up and go - it would do you good to keep a Bible around. Read it. Look at the stories of men and women, common men and women, who, through faith in God, conquered lions, stopped the violence of fire, escaped death, rose to the top, destroyed armies which were more powerful in the natural than they were, and won battles in ways which baffle the mind. You will get motivated quickly. Most of all you will realize that those who refuse to quit are those who win.

Oh, I pray to God that I can encourage you to see the value of defying the odds, of holding fast to your dreams and goals, of continued reaching, consistent pursuing and steadfast determination. Hold out until you accomplish one thing worth something to you. Get one victory under your belt. Prove to yourself that you can attain to your desire. Taste the sweetness of one victory. It will motivate you for more.

The first book I published was the hardest one for me. The first book I published was not the first book I wrote. I had written one before, but I never published it. Then I began to write others. I would get so far in them, writing chapter after chapter. Then, when it seemed as if I had writer's block and could not see what I should write next, I stopped and started another book. One day a realization hit me that I would never get my books out to the people who needed to know what I had learned through the years if I did not work on finishing what I started and then get them published. Books cannot write themselves. They cannot publish themselves. It was then that I determined to be a finisher.

So I finished my book, *"Diligence to the Things of God,"* and then looked for a publisher. I found one, self-published it, and, at this time, you are reading my eleventh book. I am just getting started. I hear books constantly rolling around in me. Inspiration comes constantly. And I give God all the glory for the ability to put pen to paper and write articles and books which can make a marked and eternal difference in the lives of others.

I am not telling you to write a book. However, I do remember a great and tremendous author once saying that everyone has at least one good book in them. But my point in emphasizing my experience as a writer in part to you is to show you the value of staying with a project, pursuing a goal, until you get the results you desire to get. I have yet to meet anyone who has accomplished a noteworthy dream that did not have to persist past pressure. Winners win because they never quit, not because they did not have the opportunity to do so. **Determination pays off.**

You are now being challenged to make something of yourself, to accomplish your goals and reach your God-ordained destiny. What are you prepared to do?

I would urge you to set your plans and vision down on paper. Then determine how you can see those purposes realized. Ask God for His wisdom and help in your ventures. Then set your sights high, and get busy working each step in the pursuit of your desires. Work at them daily. Work at them consistently. Work at them with the determination that you will not quit until you see them come to pass. When you develop this kind of a mind-set, you will discover that, not only are you going in the direction of your God-given dreams, but your dreams will become your reality.

Successful people are diligent. That is why they win in life.

Chapter Twenty Seven
The Spirit Of A Finisher

One of the most notable traits of successful people is that they are strong and effective finishers of what they undertake to accomplish.

I have emphasized the importance of becoming focused in our purpose and pursuits. This point is so vital that it bears repeating over and over again until the comprehension of what is being said sinks into our hearts and minds. The intent is that we learn what it means to keep the objective of what we are attempting to accomplish in the forefront of our thinking until the objective becomes a reality.

With this thought in mind, we will have to be aggressive in defeating mediocrity and procrastination and take bold and continuous action towards our dreams. I know that it may seem as though I am saying the same things I have already said. If this is your perception, then you are right. I am using different ways of getting the same truths and principles across, but the objective of this book is to get you busy taking action steps towards your goals, and to help you learn the value of seeing things through.

If you really want to taste the sweetness of success you will have to reach the goal. The Bible says, **"The desire accomplished is sweet to the soul." (See Proverbs 13:19)** The key word here is, "accomplished."

Have you ever attained a goal? Maybe it was to get a car or vehicle of your own. Then again, maybe your goal was to get your own house. Perhaps your goal was to save money towards a desired end, such as vacation or to buy some clothing or whatever. If you stuck with your goal long enough until it became your reality, how did you feel when you got what you were after? I believe the answer would be, **GREAT, TREMENDOUS, AWESOME.** Am I Right?

This is because when you fulfill something you set out to do - when you finish a project - it gives you a sense of accomplishment and a sense of worth and value. Even though you already know you are somebody, it makes you feel like someone who has done something worthwhile. When you and I develop the attitude and mindset of a finisher, in the midst of being misunderstood by others who are satisfied with mediocrity, we will find ourselves developing a dislike for laziness and non-accomplishment. We will so enjoy getting things done and realizing our potential, that each goal attained will give way for us to dream bigger, set greater goals, and reach higher heights.

Truly successful people never stop dreaming. They never cease to be more, to do more. Again, the desire accomplished is sweet to the soul.

As an author of over eight books, I can truly say that when each was accomplished and published it only led to me wanting to write more and release more information, as I learn it, to help more people. I absolutely love adding value to people's lives by sharing truth and principles which can lift their spirits, which can affect their hearts and minds in a positive way, which can change their very lives as they know it at the moment.

I am always thrilled when someone shares with me how one of my books has had a positive effect upon them. It makes what I do worth doing, to help another person. Now that is sweet to the soul.

Likewise, whatever your goals are, if they are worth it to you and can help and advance others, then you should be busy pushing them as far as you can. I personally believe God Almighty has a purpose for every life. You have something within, a seed of greatness which He placed in you from your mother's womb. The key to winning in life is to connect with the Creator, discover what that purpose is and then walk it out, and sometimes run it out, until it is realized.

What do you have within? What dream and passion constantly comes to your mind? Is it to write books which trigger the imagination and add value to humanity? Is it to sing songs which inspire hearts and soothes the soul? Maybe your desire is to teach people (perhaps in school). Or you may dream of running your own business of some kind, which can help people get what they want. You may desire to work in law enforcement to help keep law and order so that people may be more safe, and those who dare to practice wrong may be stopped in their tracks. Either way, the key to getting what you want and fulfilling your goals is to learn the power of being consistent so that you can reach your mark. Once you have completed one goal let it motivate you to set other goals.

Here is what I would like to suggest to you. Finish one goal you desire to reach. Celebrate the moment and experience the absolute taste of victory and success. Then go after another, and then another. Some of us have even learned how to attain more than one goal at the same time. We have come to realize that if we set our plans just right, much of what it takes people a lifetime to accomplish can be attained in short order with focus and determination.

So are you a finisher? Or have you developed the habit of starting a project, stopping midway because you face an obstacle, or perhaps because you get bored easily, only to start another, then another, and then another. No wonder you are so frustrated and depressed. If you are not attaining any of your goals, you most likely are miserable. Remember this: "Joy comes from a relationship with God. And happiness comes from the realization of completed goals."

Truly successful people are strong finishers of whatever they start. That is why they win in life.

Chapter Twenty Eight
Do You Have What It Takes

One of the most fascinating things about a truly diligent person is that he or she refuses to quit or give up until the goal is realized or the job is done.

I know that we have mentioned the power of persistence in this book several times, in various ways. But this point is so vital to you and me accomplishing our dreams and God given destiny that I believe it wise to really drive it home. Here is where, for the most part, failure occurs. People give up too soon. We look at those who attain their goals as if they are something special, as if they have some innate ability to simply outshine us all. The truth is that they are special. And so are we.

I have found that what sets winners apart is that they are willing to keep pushing while others fall away. They are determined to keep at it, going in the direction of their dreams, while others say, "It's too hard!" throw up their hands and back off. Someone has so rightly said that winners are not those who never fail, but those who never quit.

This book is written to help you develop the spirit of the winner. That's right. I want you to taste the sweetness of realizing fulfilled goals. Once you discover how to persevere you can attain the impossible with the help of the Almighty. You can become that doctor, be that best-selling author, become a professional basketball player, own your own business, or accomplish any notable task you decide to undertake. You can get the education you desire. You can go back to school, even if it involves taking night classes, and ace the exams. Nothing is impossible with God and nothing is impossible to him or her who believes.

I speak to the dreamer in you, the visionary in you. Seize your destiny. Make up your mind to go for it and never ever quit.

Here are seven keys to developing, as a friend of mine calls it, "a no quitting sense:" They are, in a nut shell, what we have already covered through-out this book.

1. Realize that you dream is possible regardless of where you came from, your background, color or financial condition at the moment.

2. Make a plan of action. Make sure it is practical enough to begin implementing so you can begin to take action immediately.

3. Count the cost. Understand that sacrifices will have to be made along the way in order to reach your goals. Be willing to make those sacrifices, keeping the end in sight.

4. Get with it. Begin to take action on your plans. Do not procrastinate any longer. Do what you can step by step, day by day.

5. Realize that challenges will come, but you must persevere and stay focused. Keep in mind what you are after and always remember to keep the main thing the main thing.

6. As things appear to get tougher, keep moving forward as best you can, praying, trusting and working. I cannot emphasize enough the importance of remaining focused at this point. Discouragement may and will attempt to set in at various stages. Things may not always go in the manner you thought they would. And discouragement will bring his cousin or brother with him named depression. Some of you may be at this point right now. This is when you feel like throwing in the towel. But if you are going to experience victory, you will have to persist. Hang in

there. Keep on keeping on. Do not quit. There are several things you can do to help you remain steadfastly focused. Read some biographies and autobiographies of those who faced challenges and overcame. This works for me. Also, you may want to ask someone for advice. A word of caution here though: make sure the person you are speaking to has a life-style which proves they know what they are speaking about.

7. Set it in your heart and soul that you will reach your goals. When you are determined to win, and refuse to quit, you will enjoy the awesome realization of fulfilled dreams.

Chapter Twenty Nine
Diligence Involves Work

Work is not a bad word.

Does that surprise you? Some people believe that work is a curse the Creator placed upon man for sinning against Him. This is simply not true. Actually, when God made man, He gave him work before He created woman. That's right. Go and read the first two chapters of Genesis for yourself. God gave man work. Then He gave him a wife. So work was given to man before sin ever existed.

Work is a good thing. And you had better embrace working, for you will never realize your goals without working and applying yourself towards them. I think some are afraid of this word called work. But if you determine to be a success and you learn the value of committing yourself to the actual pursuit of your dreams, you may astound yourself as to what can happen.

The book you desire to write will never write itself, regardless of how much you dream of doing it. The education you want to get will not be realized just by thinking about it. You can dream all day about starting your own business or learning a trade, or even becoming a singer. But somewhere along the line, you are going to have to wake up and get to work.

I am, at this writing, the author of at least nine books. The books would not have been written had I not applied myself and started typing. Actually, when I began typing I was pretty slow at it. But I kept at it. And do you know that the more I applied myself, the sooner I finished one book after the other. And I got better at typing as well.

I have found that the way to get things done is to simply determine what it will take to get it done, draw up a workable plan of action, and then get it to. Do it. Apply yourself. **Refuse to Procrastinate.**

Believe me when I say that you have it in you to reach your God given destiny. You can see your dreams come to pass. You can make it. You can do it. You can become it, whatever it is for and to you. And even if you do not get it right the first, second or third time, that is no reason to quit and give up. If, within your heart, you know that your dream is worth it, then never give up.

I realize that some people may feel as if they can sit on the sidelines and just dream and it will come to pass. But this has not been my experience. And it has not been the experience of any successful person I know or have read about. Yes, we dream. Yes, we imagine ourselves doing great things in the future. However, at some point, we wake up and get to work.

I can imagine that there are some who are reading this book right now. You have dreamed of how you would like your life to be. You have envisioned yourself being successful in one or several areas of your life. You can see yourself writing that book, making that Christian music album, getting that higher paying job, receiving that high school diploma or university degree. But the only thing hindering your success is that you have not taken action. Maybe you fear failure. Maybe you allow your mind to think that whatever you plan on doing may fail. But, as many people have said through the years, "How do you know if you never try?"

I remember the day I thought about going after my Doctorate Degree in Theology. I had already received two earned Master's Degrees. When I spoke to the University, I was told that I may be able, if I applied myself, to get it in three years. I thought to myself, "Three years?" Then the thought came, "If you don't do it now, and decide to do it later, it will still take you the same amount of time. You might as well get it done." What did I do? I took action. At this present time, I have concluded one year and started my second term. God is

Good. You will never get where you desire to go if you never get started.

I am writing to urge you to get busy doing what you need to do to get where you are attempting or desiring to go. Stop waiting on conditions to become perfect. They may never become that perfect. Do what you can, believing God that when you reach as far as you can the revelation of how to get further will be made plain to you.

Here is how King Solomon puts it:

Ecclesiastes 11:4
"He that observeth the wind shall not sow; and he that regardeth the clouds shall not reap."

May this book serve as an encouragement to you to reach for your goals and dreams with all of your heart, knowing that if you dare to believe God and have confidence in yourself and the abilities He has given you, you can accomplish much. I am pulling for you. Now get to work.

Prayer of Salvation

God loves you and has provided the gift of salvation for you. This gift is in His Son, the Lord Jesus Christ.

To receive God's precious gift, you must receive Jesus Christ as your Lord and Savior. To do so simply pray these words and mean them with your whole heart:

Oh God in Heaven. I come to You in the Name of Your Son, the Lord Jesus Christ. I am a sinner. I need a Savior. Jesus is that Savior. I believe that Jesus Christ, Your Son, died for my sins. I believe that He was buried and that You raised Him from the dead. And right now, I receive Jesus Christ as my Lord and my Savior. And because Your Word says that if I do this I would be saved, I want to thank You right now for saving me and washing my sins away in His precious blood. In Jesus Name I pray, Amen.

According to the following passage of Scripture, if you do this, you can be assured that you are now a child of God.

Romans 10: 9
"That if thou shalt confess with thy mouth the Lord Jesus, and shalt believe in thine heart that God hath raised Him from the dead, thou shalt be saved."

If you enjoyed this book please check put these other books by Sheldon D. Newton

My Name is Jealous

How To Live The Christian Life Successfully

How To Pray & Get Results

The Powerful Ministry Of Intercession

Humility & The Honor of God

Diligence to the Call Of God

Genna's Fight (A Novel)

How To Hide God's Word In Your Heart

For books, audio teaching and other material by Bishop Sheldon D. Newton, you may write to him at:

Bishop Sheldon D. Newton
P. O. Box. N. 10257
Nassau, Bahamas.
www.sheldondnewton.org

Email Sheldon D. Newton at: sheldond.newton@gmail.com

Made in the USA
Columbia, SC
21 December 2023